I loved reading the book, *NO FATHER NO EXCUSES.* The knowledge that Chris has regarding being a fatherless child, gave him the strength to be a father to a fatherless child. There are several men in today's society that are facing open wounds of being fatherless, and I am one of them. After reading this book, it allowed me to gain a deeper insight and to know I am not alone. My father went to prison when I was 3 years old and returned home when I was 22. "No father, no excuses" woke up and spoke to my spirit man. My father and I went from absolutely no relationship, to talking 3-5 times a week. I highly encourage all men to read this and allow the words to speak to them. Thank you, Chris Chavez, for the wisdom you shared; and thank you for inspiring the next generation. You will not regret it!

—**Michael Meadows**, Grambling University—Former Student Body President

I first met Chris Chavez in 2014. Since that time, we've shared time, thoughts, frustrations, prayers and ideas almost weekly. I'm most excited about "No Father, No Excuses because I literally watched it being written in his life over that last seven years. The lessons you will read in these pages were prayed about, researched and lived out while the Lord taught him to rise above being fatherless. In these pages, you will find a guide from someone who gets it. Chris is a fatherless father who relied on the Heavenly Father to teach him to be a Godly father. The way he is raising his five children can change our generation. I am the father of three young men ages 27, 21 and 20 and I will be revisiting some discussions with this resource.

I'm grateful for the gift and the anointing on his life to express how to do life in an applicable, relatable format through No Father – No Excuses.

—**Matt Miller**, Pastor, Bethany Worship Center

From the moment I opened the book, I was hooked. As a single mother raising a son, this book gave me the chance to see what things I could miss giving my son because he is not being raised by his father. This book, while frightening at what my son might lack as a man, is also, eye opening and informative. Certain sections are now dog-eared, folded back and full of notes, my son and I are discussing these issues now. I think we can all appreciate that Chris Chavez is a straight shooter. He is a Christian man full of biblical principles and knowledge, yet this book is so practical you can begin to change your thinking and thought process immediately. You will find yourself nodding your head in agreement and wishing you had known that sooner (like the cash car, school and how to manage your money). This is a must read for any man who did not grow up with a father and for the single mothers raising sons.

—**Hilarie Rock**, author of *Girl, He's Got You: A Single Mother's Devotional*

Men have not been given the power to abuse but to protect, empower their families purpose and identity. Men are empowered to stop blaming. Power to deal with current situations. The power to father!

There are men who blame the past, become powerless and never man up for their current mentality. There are some men that not only step up and take on the responsibility of other biological parents' children. It is hard pill to swallow when accepting responsibility to move on. *No Father No Excuses*, has to be an important part of your mindset. This is a must read! Thank you, Chris Chavez, for inspiring and empowering the future generation!

—**Pablo De Leon**, Author. Actor. Athlete. Producer

Hunkie Cooper, College Football Coach, Father of three boys and three girls, former Professional athlete that lost my father at 14 years of age and became a father at 18 years of age.

I really loved reading *No Father, No Excuses* because the book derived from Chris's personal knowledge. I say knowledge and not information because information could be given as bad information, misinformation or good information but knowledge is from your own personal trials, tribulation and experiences.

This book allowed me to look back over my own life and the life of other young men that I have coached, mentored or crossed paths with and had lost their father through no fault of their own.

In sports we pray before we lead our teams and young men into battle and that prayer always started with "OUR FATHER" but what about the young men who never had a father and didn't know what fatherly love was or never had a man to show them how to be a man.

This book introduces you to the best father anyone can ever have and how you can build and have a personal relationship with him. This book takes you from childhood days, throughout his youth, into his professional career, collegiate career and gives great examples of how faithful, just and forgiving God is when you trust his word and have a professional relationship with him.

I highly recommend *No Father No Excuses* to anyone who is becoming a father, never had a father or wants to become a better father and man of God.

—**Hernandez "Hunkie" Cooper**, San Diego St Asst.
Football Coach, AFL Hall of Fame 2011,
2x AFL Ironman of the Year

NO FATHER NO EXCUSES

LESSONS FROM A FATHERLESS FATHER

CHRIS CHAVEZ

No Father No Excuses
Lessons From A Fatherless Father

Published by Wyden Publishing in Houston, TX

To contact Chris or inquire about book orders, go to chrischavez.net.

eISBN: 978-1-63296-467-0
ISBN: 978-1-63296-468-7

This book is dedicated to the memory of Keith Bacon;
a great friend known by few in this world but
well known in heaven. He was a soul winner,
never gave up and always trusted God.

ACKNOWLEDGEMENTS

This book was put together from the countless lessons of my life. Along the way I gathered great friends that I know at any time I can call and they will answer. Thanks to Dana Nollette, Jim Juergens, Joe Rodden, Caesar Hermogeno, Matt Miller, Morgan Proudfoot, Randy Griffin and Pablo Contreras. And a special thanks to Rich Cass, who prayed the prayer asking God to give me some buds.

To The Reader

Walking into a church service with no real Christian friends I heard a loud voice call me. It was the voice of a college drinking buddy, Dustin Smith. Across the large foyer he said "Chavez!!!!! Man, if you are in church, everybody should be in church!" So true; if God pulled me from my sins, you are well within His reach.

TABLE OF CONTENTS

Acknowledgements iv

Chapter 1—Blind Men Can't See 1

Chapter 2—You're The Problem 11

Chapter 3—A Fool And His Money 21
Wants And Needs *25*
Quick Money *28*
Car Debt *31*
Student Loans *40*
Buying A Home *46*
Saving *53*
Investing *59*
Giving *63*
Life After Death *66*
Credit Cards *70*
Insurance *73*
Final Thoughts On Money *76*

Chapter 4—Chasing Ghosts 78

Chapter 5—School Daze 89
The Game Is Changing *91*
So What Do You Do? *97*

Chapter 6—Dear Mama 104

Chapter 7—Females and Friends 112
What should I do? *117*
Why change? *118*
Friends *120*
Family *125*

Chapter 8—Discover Who You Really Are 127
Final Words *139*

Chapter 9—Gotta Work If You Wanna Eat 140
Find Meaning In Your Work *142*
Navigating The Workplace *146*
Injustice At Work *149*
Office Politics *154*
Accomplishment *158*
Final Words On Work *161*

Chapter 10—Decisions Make The Man 164
Bad Decisions *165*
What Makes A Good Decision? *167*
Making Good Decisions *170*

Chapter 11—Repairing and Rebuilding 179
Step 1: Start With Your Father *183*
Step 2: Start Rebuilding *188*

Chapter 12—One Life: Leave A Path Not A Legacy 193
One Life *198*
Head To A Mirror And Tell Yourself The Truth *200*

Epilogue 202

Nuggets 205

Resources 214

About the Author 217

CHAPTER 1

BLIND MEN CAN'T SEE

A little-known rule of thumb when headed to a job interview—make sure you take a clean copy of your resume and always make sure your last will and testament are up to date.

In the summer of 1976, my father drove south on US Hwy 84 to a job interview in Houston, Texas. He didn't even make it 50 miles from home. A northbound truck passing where he was not supposed to pass hit my father head on. My father died instantly in that auto accident, leaving my 31-year-old mom a widow with four kids aged 12, 8, 6, and 2. I was the 6-year-old, my brothers were older than me and my sister was the 2-year-old. I turned 7 two months later, and to this day I have no memories of my father. I can't recall anything. So, I grew up without a father's guidance. I got into trouble continually at school without a father's discipline, played sports without a father's presence or encouragement, went away to college without a father's advice, started a career without a father's input. I was married without a father's blessing. And today as I write this, I am the father of five and a fatherless father.

Oh, I have seen pictures of my father and me and I know who he is, I just don't remember him. For many of you, I am sure you have a different version of a familiar story that know all too well. A story that leaves you with memories of no memories. In the end, whether your father left and never came back, died before you were born, divorced your mom and cast you off along with her, was emotionally unavailable or whatever the situation you endured, the result is the same—you grew up fatherless. This book was written for you and those all around you that grew up fatherless.

Now, it may not seem odd that I don't remember my father until you consider that he died the summer before I entered the second grade. So when I say I don't remember my dad, that does not mean I don't have memories of him. Those memories for whatever reason are locked away in a place I can't access. Even though my father was married to my mom, living with us and a part of my daily life, I don't remember him. I don't remember anything he might have taught me, said to me, done with me, or recall any family event. Not so with my older brothers. They have all the memories and the pain of losing what they remember—a dad. My brother Jeff once asked me if I remember going to the officer's club on the Air Force base we lived on and I said I remember going but I don't remember dad being there. It just doesn't make sense to him that I can't remember things that he remembers with absolute clarity. We are only two years apart, so I get why he is confused. If you have any children in your life, imagine if you were gone and they just couldn't remember you. Odd, huh?

In retrospect, it all makes sense though. Losing a parent is a traumatic event and the mind copes with trauma in various ways. There is a book called *The Body Keeps Score* which really is a great resource that I highly recommend. The book really digs into how any trauma effects the body in ways we don't recognize and brings into focus how much we really need healing from past trauma. That book explains that most people are dealing with some sort of childhood trauma, but they just don't know it. As a result, most don't seek to have that trauma healed. I can't say I intentionally set out to work through that trauma, but I know that in following Christ much of that trauma has melted away. Yet regardless of all the healing in my life, those memories of my dad are still lost.

But even though I grew up without an earthly father, I did grow up with a Heavenly Father. The way I see it now, I was gifted my 'amnesia' so I could walk through my life, make mistakes, grow, make bigger mistakes, and grow so much more. All of this may have happened so you, my fatherless brothers, could glean lessons of what not to do and lessons you wish your father would have taught you. So many people want to tell you what to do but just as important is to learn what *not* to do. Pain was sown into my life only to one day produce a harvest of life lessons. I'm not saying God killed my father so I could write a book. What I am saying is that He has made all things work together for the good of those who love him. And to the non-Christian, I am saying that since this book is written to be practical, there is much for you to glean because I have already travelled the road you are on now and I know the pitfalls and landmines, so I can help you to make better decisions.

A father wound is not a clinical term as far as I know but it is a phrase used in the church and society all the time. A father wound is the inner hurt or pain caused by either the absence of a father or the direct pain he caused in a child's life. It can be the source of behavioral, mental, and relationship issues that can plague a person for years, if not their entire life. For many of you, that father wound happened because he was not present, not a good father, physically present but emotionally absent, abusive, demanding, or just had nothing to give.

Now, most men who grew up without fathers have some type of father wound.

So many of you have stories that have shaped your lives. Some of you have made vows because of his actions, things like, "I'll never be like him." Others of you just wasted years of your life until you finally stumbled upon a path that felt right. In fact, I know of a guy who pursued education all the way through law school, yet today he doesn't practice law. I asked him about it and he simply said he had a dad, but he wasn't a very good one, so it took him a while before he knew who he was. He wasted a lot of years figuring out who he was all on his own.

I on the other hand always felt blessed because, since my dad was killed in a car wreck, it wasn't his fault. He didn't wound me and I never questioned God as to why, I just accepted it. And the more I have interacted with other guys throughout the years, I am more thankful that I'm fatherless due to an auto accident. Being fatherless because of a biological father's failure just wreaks havoc on a man's life. It can stir up so much bitterness, anger, and resentment and destroy personal relationships, not to mention how having a poor father affects how one views God as father.

I have a hope that guys like you will glean some foundational building blocks that will guide you toward a godly manhood that will bless your wife, kids, community, and the Kingdom of God. This book is not intended to be some autobiography to inspire or encourage. This book is meant to be practical, giving you tools you can use for the rest of your life.

The personal stories I share are mostly of failure just to reveal to the actual consequences of those mistakes. So often I have heard sermons calling men to "grow up" or telling them to stop being boys and to be men but I rarely hear them tell you how. I'm not talking about something "manly" like changing a tire or shaving, I'm talking about how to view the different areas of life and the practical things needed to navigate that area. Being a man requires living life through a certain lens, not just having facts. You can read a book explaining the rules of basketball, but it won't compare to being taught *how* to play a real game where opponents are trying to stop you, counter your actions, and impose their plan on your team. If you just have book knowledge, you really can't play the game.

Here are two great examples from my own life. When I was 35, I was hanging out with a friend of mine about the same age who just bought a house. Now, although we were both looking for jobs, neither of us had jobs at the time and I distinctly remember asking him, "How did you buy a house and you don't even have a job?" His reply was matter of fact, saying he put it on an "arm" and would change that when he landed a job. I didn't ask a follow up question. Why? Because he answered my question and I honestly didn't know what I should say or ask as a follow up.

Fast forward about ten years later, and my wife and I are having a great date at Papasita's. We got a break from the kids, got some bacon wrapped shrimp, enjoyed a great margarita, and had a great conversation. For some reason during dinner, I asked her what made her think to buy a house when she was in her mid 20's, years before we got married. I asked because it just seemed extraordinary for a 26-year-old to own a house.

So when I asked my friend and my wife about buying a house, I was not totally ignorant. By age 31, I had an undergrad degree in finance, an MBA, was a military veteran, had worked a financial planner which included passing the Series 6, 7, and 63 exams and completed courses toward my CFP (Certified Financial Planner). It wasn't that I didn't have knowledge. It was that I didn't have the lens to make the knowledge applicable to my life. If I did, then I would have understood that he said ARM (Adjustable Rate Mortgage) not just heard the word 'arm'. I had book knowledge, but they knew how to play the game. That is called wisdom.

See, I had all the financial information so I could be successful and have a nice house and things. I just didn't know the first thing about how to actually get a house. People in my family didn't own houses. Rich people had houses, specifically white people are the ones that I knew had houses. After my father died, we moved to where my mother's family lived in East Texas. I grew up in 13 different houses and apartments in that small town of 17,000 people. We were renters and we moved all the time because that is what renters do. I remember when one of my uncles actually bought a house. To me it was a big deal. Looking back, one might just consider it a starter home having three bedrooms, no frills, and about 1,600 square feet. But to me, in my mind, he did something special.

But all those years later, after all that financial education, having obtained a job working as a financial planner with the ability to do a zero-down VA loan and before the housing crash when anyone could buy a house, it never entered my mind to buy a house. I'm serious; it never entered my mind to buy a house. It never entered my mind because when I looked in the mirror. I didn't see a homeowner. I saw a guy who was good at math but didn't know how to navigate life with purpose. I didn't even know the questions to ask. I just gathered the information the culture told me to acquire, assumed everything would just happen, and I would get where I wanted.

Knowledge is power only when you understand how to wield it.

That is why the Bible says get wisdom. Wisdom is higher than knowledge. Wisdom gives insight into how and when to use knowledge. Wisdom typically comes from God through fathers (see the book of Proverbs).

The education system just gives knowledge so that it all I acquired. I just didn't know I needed something more.

I grew up in a small town that had two school districts. One school district was rural and had all the working-class families, and the other district had all the white-collar families. Up to the 10th grade, I went to school in the rural, country school and to my knowledge, none of my friend's parents had college degrees; they were just good working-class people. And we are talking the 70's and 80's so you may not understand it, but college was not on the average working-class families' radar like it is today. Needless to say, being engulfed in a blue-collar culture didn't provide a path towards a life I saw for myself.

In the 10th grade, I changed schools for sports and my world was changed overnight. I grew up playing soccer and I never remember playing on a team with my school friends. My soccer friends were all kids from the other school, the rich kids. These kids had different lives. I remember going to practice back in junior high at one of their houses and that family had their own tennis court. By no means did it stir up jealousy or anything like that, it was just the beginning of me learning that there is another world out there.

During my high school days, I was much more intentional about figuring out life. It was not a concerted or calculated plan; it was just something inside me that knew that I needed to find my path to success. I was watching and learning from all my classmates. At the time all I wanted was to be a success, to be someone. It wasn't the stuff the other kids had; it was just the simple fact that in my eyes their world would take me places I wanted to go.

So yes, I desired a house someday, a big house among other things, but for me "someday" was not a definable time because I just didn't have the lens to get there. My soccer friends had parents who instilled a different lens for life in them. Life isn't about gaining possessions or having a great job. Life is about so much more. Of course, along the way, there are the purchases of things like cars, houses, land, and beyond. I learned the phrase "Begin with the end in mind" from my time in the military and the phrase is correct. Having a destination helps determines first steps and all the steps along the way. It also helps you to formulate a plan.

They say having a goal without a plan is just a wish. For much of my life, I had a bunch of wishes and no goals. All because without a father, there was nobody to teach me how to navigate life with intention. I didn't have him informing me of how the world works. Seriously, how would a Mexican kid from an east Texas town of 17,000 people know the first thing about buying a house? I am sure that if you are reading this book, there are plenty of things you wish you were taught when you were younger, things that pave an intentional path leading towards sure goals. My stories about the purchase of a house are meant to point to the real problem – my childhood is what gave me my lens for life. And with a poor lens, I was playing checkers while others were playing chess. I wasn't just behind in the game, I was playing the wrong game.

This book will address all those things that a man needs know, have, and do to be a man today, and specifically a godly man. **It isn't just knowledge that fatherless men need; it is a new lens to view life through.** Fatherless men are blind but the only real way to see is to give them a new lens for life. That lens needs to give direction on money, education, relationships, careers, and other aspects of life including the healing needed from not having a father or being wounded by your father. Along with that lens I also hope to give some practical help, hacks and direction to help you avoid life's pitfalls. If they are really honest with themselves, people will tell you that it is their own personal decisions that have led to their own demise.

This is written from a Christian perspective but most of the helps, hints, and suggestions are universal in nature. This book is for you if you grew up without a father's instruction, whether you are a believer in Jesus Christ or not. If you are looking for a Christian Apologetic for biblical manhood, this book is not it. This is a book meant to help all men, both believer and unbeliever. My invitation is to follow along, learn from my mistakes and the lessons I have learned, and you will see life with a new lens.

CHAPTER 2

YOU'RE THE PROBLEM

William Shakespeare, *A Winter's Tale, Act III, Scene 3*

> *SHEPHERD*
> *"I wish that the ages between sixteen and twenty-three didn't exist, or that young men would spend them asleep. Otherwise there is nothing between those ages but getting girls pregnant, acting dishonestly toward their elders, stealing, fighting. . . ."*

Shakespeare penned those words over 400 years ago, but he absolutely had it right. Guys between 16 and 23 would be better off asleep than allowed to live among us. In today's world that time in men's life is just full of countless mistakes and you can count me among that number. We just don't get it and I would contend that those mistakes we make during that time period haunt many of us for the rest of our lives. I have told many a teenager that this is the smartest time in their lives because right now they believe they know everything. It is sad that it will take a good 20 years of life humbling them before they realize they don't really know anything. And there lies the problem – if it isn't put into us before age 16 and we don't listen to anyone older and wiser than us, we foolishly tend to have to learn from our own mistakes. Rather than listening to someone who has been there before, we ignore the voices that "just don't understand."

This youthful exuberance combined with a total lack of how the world really works is supercharged by the fact that many of us didn't have a father to help us. Growing up, I was the only one I knew that was fatherless but at 27 I discovered my life to be totally uncommon. I joined the US Army at 27. I promised to serve four years and they promised to pay back my mountain of school loan debt ($45K). I did both my basic training and job training in Ft. Jackson, South Carolina. My units were Charlie 2-13 and Echo 3-69. Shout out to Drill Sergeant Williams and Drill Sergeant Stewart wherever you are. At the end of each of those trainings are graduation ceremonies in full Class A attire. That means we put on our formal military suits and that includes wearing ties.

I had absolutely no problem tying a tie. I didn't have a father to teach me, but I distinctly remember kneeling down at the edge of my closet and learning how to tie a tie from my oldest brother's Cub Scout book. I must have been 11 or 12 and there really was no occasion driving me to learn; I just wanted to learn how to tie a tie. Now fast forward to my graduation ceremonies, I had no problem getting ready. I taught myself as a kid, so I had tied my own ties for years. The trick is really knowing at what length to start the ends depending on your specific height. Tall guys have to start in a spot totally different from short guys. Once you have that down, you can tie a tie for anyone and that is just what I did. I tied dozens and dozens of ties for those graduation ceremonies. I went all through the barracks tying ties for soldiers that could not tie a tie. All of them were fatherless. That summer was the first time I realized how many other men were fatherless just like me.

It isn't like learning to tie a tie is the pinnacle of manhood or even a measure of any sort. Today you can learn all that type of stuff on YouTube but if you could enter my memories and see the faces of all those soldiers that felt inept and totally lost, you would feel burdened for young men everywhere. These men just completed the basic training that equipped them to deploy to a war and yet they still lacked the skills needed to go to a job interview let alone all the tools needed for manhood. Without a father, each man was left to build himself into a man, whatever that meant to him.

Moving into active duty and living in the barracks from ages 27-31, I saw firsthand these fatherless soldiers make mistake after mistake. 40 ounces, CD's, clothes, and jewelry dominated most everyone's major expenses. And outside of Ft. Hood is Killeen, Texas where there are countless businesses whose sole income comes from fleecing young soldiers, making it simple to draft their credit payments directly from their paychecks. Cars, rims, clothes, stereos, anything a young soldier with a steady paycheck could want.

I knew one guy whose paycheck was $8.00 every two weeks because the rest went to pay his creditors.

Whose fault is it? The businesses? The military's? The soldier's? The answer is the responsibility lies with the soldier, but the fault lies with a father who never taught his son how to navigate life. Even at 27 and having already lived that mindless pleasure-seeking life in college, I still made my own mistakes. Sure, I lived smarter than most and even though the Army was paying off my $45K in student loans, I still accumulated another $5K in new student loans for a master's degree and about 7K in credit card debt. Without a father, it is 2 steps forward 1 step back and that is if you are lucky.

I've always likened becoming a man to creating a statue. There are two ways to build a statue. You can begin with clay and build from the ground up or you can begin with a piece of stone and chip away at it until the image you have in your mind is revealed. Either way, you must begin with the end in mind. Without a father, little by little, from the ground up I built myself into what I thought a man was or should be. Admittedly, I built myself into a man based upon my culture informed mind and my own earthly desires. In the end, God in his loving mercy took control and began chipping away at all I built. He surgically chipped away at all that I built up; supernaturally reshaping me into his desires. And lest you forget, the foundation is the most important part of building anything. **Note to men everywhere: Always build on rock, never sand. That means you better be building with Jesus as a foundation for anything.**

For men who currently have kids, I have four boys under my care I am now much more intentional. I don't just take the clay God gave me and start shaping my boys into who I think they should become. Instead, I fully realize that God is the one who knows these boys better than I ever will. My job is to inquire of God how He wants me to shape each of my sons. Yes, there are characteristics that all men should possess but each son was uniquely created by God to do good works. My job is to intentionally shape them and form them as God wants them. My hope is that as they become men, there is less for God to chip away and He can spend His time polishing them instead.

Christian men need to understand that if you don't learn God's ways, He will come and teach you them in love. And that same love will also tear down what you built. He saved me early in life but as I said, I built myself into what I thought was a man. Thus, upon my repenting and returning to God, He began disciplining me for my years of disobedience. For five straight years, He undid what I had built myself into. I remember sitting in my car in front of a high school and reading Jeremiah 30. In that chapter, God tells Israel of the pain they are about to endure for their continued disobedience. He is talking to Israel, but I heard Him tell me the same thing He said to them. Israel had been disobedient for years and God told them that painful discipline was coming. Similarly, God told me that I knew better and that the pain of discipline was coming. Then He began to take His chisel and strike blow upon blow to what I had built. Unlike most prodigals, He didn't call me back to him as I was eating with the pigs. I had achieved all that I had ever planned in my life as a child. I had arrived and I arrived my way. That said, God matched my pride with humbling after humbling experience until I really embraced that my place is a place of obedience. Wherever you are, whatever life stage you find yourself in as you read this book, take note and learn that the sooner you learn his ways, the sooner you move toward becoming a man of God.

If you are like me, the truth is that most of your problems today are because of bad decisions you made and the shaky foundations you built upon between the ages of 16 and 23, especially the financial problems. Studies have shown that boys that grow up without fathers are less confident or insecure[1] (NCBI study). That insecurity effects relationships, what risks we won't take, and even how much risk we will take to cover up that insecurity.

Lacking a father leaves deep wounds and glaring holes in a man's ability to navigate life.

Men who grew up without fathers also lack the ability to delay gratification.[2] And on and on it goes. Some of you are successful because you think you are fearless but as you get older you will come to understand that you were actually scared and that is why you have a measure of success. Allowing fear to motivate you feeds a beast you can't tame. Fear leads to anxiety and that anxiety will lead to depression. This self-actualization usually comes with age, but my hope is that as you read this book, you allow your subconscious

1. https://www.ncbi.nlm.nih.gov/pmc/articles/PMC3904543/
2. https://thepsychologist.bps.org.uk/volume-29/june/absent-fathers-and-sexual-strategies

to speak to you. The sooner you come to grips with what not having a father has done to you, the sooner you can heal. Not having a father is like a cancer with tentacles that reach so many areas of our lives. This can have disastrous effects on marriages, relationships, finances, and, most importantly, our faith.

Without a godly father, most boys won't know who they are. Not knowing who you are is a deep insecurity that will manifest in pretending to be someone else or trying to become someone outside of who God made you to be. Any success in becoming that imaginary person will lead to an emptiness in our souls because it just isn't what we were created to do.

One of the saddest examples is a former athlete, Todd Marinovich. You can look up ESPN's *30 for 30* video documentary on him. His father bred him to be an NFL quarterback. His whole life was orchestrated to get to the NFL and he eventually was a first round pick, only to have life come crashing down on him. Deep down he was not living a life he was created for. Speaking of his ability to play quarterback, I remember him saying something like, "One of the things I struggled with is, if you are good at something, does that mean you are meant to do it?" His words were weighty and profound. It isn't a small thing to become an NFL quarterback. There are only 32 men in the world that hold the title NFL starting quarterback. Here was one of them that *could* do it, but he didn't *want* to do it.

One of the biggest problems of men who grew up without a father is not knowing your identity. If you don't know who you are then you will grow into who you think you need to be, or worse, what others want you to be. But what does that mean? How do you quantify not knowing who you are? One way to measure this is to just look at statistics of what happens to boys without fathers in their lives.

Young men who grow up in homes without fathers are twice as likely to end up in jail as those who come from traditional two-parent families, even when other factors such as race, income, parent education, and urban residence were held constant.[3] Children living in female-headed families with no spouse present had a poverty rate of 47.6%, over four times the rate of children in married-couple families (10.9%).[4] And according to the Bureau of Justice Statistics, the number of children with an incarcerated father grew 79% between 1991 and 2007. Black fathers accounted for nearly half (46%) of all children with an incarcerated father.[5] I could go on and on, but this is something that we all know—having a father makes a difference in the lives of children.

If you are reading this then you may feel like a statistic, but you are not. Subconsciously your relationships, work ethic, decisions, and even employment history have been affected by not having a father. It doesn't take a rocket scientist to know this and my greatest desire is to help you move past the problem and give you solutions to everyday

---

3. Harper C, McLanahan SS. Cited in Father Absence and Youth Incarceration. *Journal of Research on Adolescence.* 2004.

4. *U.S. Department of Health & Human Services (2012). Information on poverty and income statistics: A summary of 2012 current population survey data. Retrieved from: http://aspe.hhs.gov/hsp/12/PovertyAndIncomeEst/ib.cfm*

5. Glaze, L.E., & Maruschak, L.M. (2010). Parents in prison and their minor children. Washington, D.C.: Bureau of Justice Statistics.

life. The only people this book will help are those that can admit they could use help. Every NFL rookie knows how to play football, but they don't know how to be a professional with the ability to handle the speed of the game on the field along with everything off the field that comes with being in the NFL. Thus, many talented athletes have been cut or have not reached their potential and, despite earning millions, left the game broke. If you think the rules of life don't apply to you and that your talent will carry you, then you won't listen. I pray God gives you ears to hear as we walk together through this book.

Even as I discuss the problems caused by fatherlessness, I want to give you something practical. When I talked about being driven or motivated by fear, I talked about it leading to anxiety and depression. With that said, I want to tell you the antidote. The antidote is embracing the untainted love that God has for you. Once you really and truly embrace that you are enough because Jesus sacrifice was enough. You will never fear man again. There is absolutely nobody who can judge you and the one who can judge you is praying for you. (Romans 8:31-35). Being motivated by love and gratitude is the exact opposite of being motivated by fear. Memorize that verse and meditate on it daily until it takes roots and give you wings. If you are not a believer, don't worry. The rest of this book will help you in many practical earthy ways but know that until you are free from the grips of what men in this world think about you, fear will influence you. Think about somebody who is totally transparent about their past life with their spouse, but they have one big secret they didn't share. Yes, they are known but their world is vulnerable because at any moment she might find out. And when she does, he will have to wonder if she will still love them. That man never feels at rest.

As I write this chapter, I am 50 years old. To some that seems old but to me it seems like yesterday when I was in the 4th grade riding my bike through the neighborhood. Growing up in small town USA during the 70's and 80's means that life was completely different than yours. I don't recall one friend in my neighborhood whose parents were divorced. That world just didn't know divorce and fatherlessness. That left me in a unique position to learn things that I hope turn into great benefit for you.

CHAPTER 3

A FOOL AND HIS MONEY

Just because you can afford the payment doesn't mean you can afford to buy it.

I want to add as much value as I can in this book and in my estimation, talking about money is a must. So instead of drilling deeper into hearts and minds, I want to take a hard left and jump into the practical and talk about money. First things first, money is spiritual no doubt about it. When I say it is spiritual, I am saying wisdom is needed to handle money, not math skills. Math is physical. You don't need wisdom to do math, you just need to learn to follow the steps. Think about it: a child could be a math prodigy because math is a science, it is objective, it is factual ($A^2 + B^2 = C^2$). Money is not a science. Money is governed by wisdom and wisdom doesn't grow on trees. Wisdom is earned, learned, sought after, and handed down by those that possess it. The sooner you can let God direct you in money the better. He doesn't need your money. Money is given to get greed out of you and to help you learn His ways. It is more blessed to give than receive but you can't give what you don't have.

In Genesis 1:26 God said He made man to have dominion over the earth. In essence, He created man to manage and govern over all the resources on the earth. That means if you want to live as you are created and designed to live then you need to rule over your resources. So if you can't pay your light bill or are buried in consumer debt it means you have a spiritual problem to fix, not a monetary problem. You can get a big pay raise, inherit a windfall, or win the lottery but you will still have the same problem: you won't possess the ability to take dominion or rule over your resources. Eventually you'll be back in the same financial place as before because you will still make the same decisions that led to crushing consumer debt.

Being rich or wealthy is not what this section is about. This section is about how to handle money so you can have enough to live your life freely and freely share with others. That being said, handling money well is necessary for every level of income. And how one handles money will also determine how easily one navigates his daily life regardless of economic status. My ultimate hope is not that you would be rich but rather you would be able to handle money with wisdom so you will have something to share. To get that wisdom, you have to start in the same place I did: the place of humility. But don't be like me. I was humbled. Don't follow my prideful path. Humble yourself lest God humble you.

As I mentioned earlier, *I* got to the place *I* wanted in life and *I* did it my way. I received my MBA while I was in the military and when I got out of the military, I landed a dream job. A financial planning firm in Ft. Worth, Texas hired me as a financial planner and to be their next partner. There wasn't anyone in front of me and nobody behind me; I was their guy. The plan was to work for them 5 years, the senior partner would retire, and then I would come aboard as the newest partner . . . just like that. There was no cold calling people or trying to earn new business. In fact, I never once even picked up the phone to call anyone I knew to try to get their business. I can't convey to you how much of a dream job this opportunity was. But God loved me too much to let me live a life constructed on a foundation of pride. Fast forward about a year and a half and I felt God asking me to leave, and just like that about two months later, I left that dream job.

I don't know if you noticed but I didn't say I left that job for another one. That is because I didn't. I left that job and for the next couple of years I just found different ways to make money. It was an all-out assault on my self-made master's degree having, my way living, no counsel seeking, pride. I sold plasma, I washed cars at a car rental agency, I tried manual labor, whatever God gave me to do. I even stumbled upon a new skill not usually necessary for a degreed professional. I learned to hydrate before giving plasma. If you properly hydrate your body before selling your plasma, it takes less time. God is no respecter of persons. He will humble anyone at any time and in any way. Most of the time I didn't have much money after leaving that dream job. A couple of awesome brothers provided me rent free housing. Otherwise, I probably would have gone under.

But here is where the rubber meets the road when it comes to humility or being humbled. One night my mom called me and told me that her water heater went out in the trailer in which she was living. If I had my old job, I would have taken care of that myself. Instead I just cried and complained to God. I'm talking, I literally cried saying, "If I had my old job I could take care of this and now I can't even take care of my mom." I felt useless. How could a grown man not be able to help his mother in her time of need? But the next day she called and said somebody got her a new water heater and then somebody else was going to install it for free. As soon as she told me that, I sensed God saying, "I don't need your help, just do what I tell you to do." He would go on to do that through several situations during that time and each time, He would say "I don't need your help, just do what I tell you to do."

For years God provided for my needs and that started my journey of learning that I don't need money; God has plenty of that. What I needed was to see the world the way He sees it and the humility to keep pursuing the wisdom that informs on how to handle money. So as we delve into money, please, please understand that money is spiritual and you need wisdom to manage it.

To receive wisdom, you must humble yourself and seek to learn even when you think you don't have anything to learn.

If you read this section without humility, you will definitely leave yourself open to mistakes that you will regret. God didn't give a laundry list of do's and don'ts that will help you navigate our current world, so I am not saying that if you disagree with anything I mention that you disagree with God. But what I am saying is that outside of a few situations, most of this is beneficial for all of you. Be careful not to automatically include yourself in the 'this doesn't apply to me' group. Pride always tells us that we are different and the rules don't apply to us.

Wants And Needs

How you govern money every day comes down to wants and needs. You need electricity but you want cable. You need toothpaste but you want mouthwash. As a man, you will need to really categorize wants and needs. It will help you budget, plan, and enjoy. Part of life is enjoying it. There is nothing wrong with going on a ski trip. Just plan, save, and enjoy without even a twinge of guilt. God wants you to enjoy. Your handling of money is not a zero-sum game where every dollar you spend on yourself robs from someone else. That is not how the world works. God has not set it up where, if you enjoy a movie, an orphan on the other side of the world doesn't eat. You can be a giver and still enjoy doing something that costs money. You just need to embrace God's goodness without forgetting that money is spiritual. Wisdom will help you know when to enjoy a want or when to forgo that want for someone else's need.

Growing up, I didn't have a good understanding of wants versus needs. When you don't have abundance, it is easy for wants and needs get grouped together. I needed to pay my tuition but I also needed to go out to the bar so I could have fun. For me those needs were the same in value. What's the point of college if I can't enjoy it, right? Ignorance. Without a father, most boys won't know how to separate wants and needs in an effective way. The short term wants become needs because the future does not weigh on young men. Young men by virtue of biology can't even fully grasp long term consequences. Medically speaking the brain doesn't even fully develop until age 25 and it directly effects a male's ability to consider long term consequences.[6] Auto insurance rates are higher for youths, and even higher still for males.

Brothers, being intentional about what is truly a need and a want isn't as cut and dry as you might think. Sure, electricity vs cable is simple but what about other things? For instance, if you work from home as a video editor, having high speed internet just might be a need. There is a difference between wanting to stream movies and paying more for high-speed internet and somebody who needs it for their job. You need to be honest with yourself. You will make errors like anyone else but if you don't start seeing life's daily decisions as the means to what your tomorrow will be, you will wake up 60 years old living in the consequences of your choices. What is worse, those you love will also be living in the consequences of your choices.

The real key to making wants versus needs work out practically is to always live below your means. At any point in time that you lack the ability to save, then you are probably spending above your needs. Even when you are up to your eyeballs in debt, you still should be able to save. Saving must be a need. If I could go back in time and change how I

---

6. https://www.ncbi.nlm.nih.gov/pmc/articles/PMC3621648/

allocated my income I would do whatever I needed to do in order to live on 80% of my income or less.

Most financial programs talk about creating a budget. A budget is just a financial word for a plan. You have to learn to plan what you do with your money. Most will hear the word budget and think of some penny pincher trying to account for every penny or somebody with very little money that absolutely needs to account for every penny. Both of those are totally inaccurate. As I mentioned, a budget is just a plan. Billionaires don't just spend, invest or give without a plan. They didn't become billionaires without planning. It doesn't matter if they started as house flippers with a tiny investment, there is always a budget and a plan. If you are living without some sort of budget you are failing to plan and as the old saying goes, failing to plan is planning to fail. (Proverbs 24:27)

Now the tendency for most men is to automatically agree in their heart and then turn around and do it on their own. Most men's first thought is not "How can I get help?" Thus, I'd encourage all of you to find a program and follow their lead. If you are a reader, *Clever Girl Finance* by Bola Solunbi is a resource I would highly recommend. Don't let the name fool you, it is absolutely a book for a man to read. It is clear, well written, and covers most everything needed. It is not unmanly to seek help; it is actually the wisest thing you can do. If you were already good with money, people would be calling you for advice today. Humility asks for help. You won't be able to really move forward with money until your *wants* and *needs* are in order. Seems like a simple step but the fundamentals are always the foundation for anything.

Quick Money

Quick money is never a viable answer in manhood. It always seems like low hanging fruit but it is rotten. There will be times when somebody has a plan or opportunity, even legal ones, that seems like easy money. Listen, hard work is always necessary in success. There are no shortcuts and if you think you have found one, don't keep lying to yourself. Run, put your head down, get to work, and never look back. I don't bring up quick money because I believe it is always illegal. The problem is with your mindset or how you view things. The eye set on quick money just reveals that even if you had the money, you probably don't know what to do with it and certainly will not plan to consistently generate wealth after the quick money runs out

In the spring semester of my freshman year of college my roommate flashed $1,500 in 100-dollar bills. Now, he was 21 and vastly more experienced in life than I was at the time. I grew up in small town USA in the 70's and 80's well before the internet made the world small. Growing up I really don't know how we became aware of anything. Somehow news trickled down from NYC and LA to the small local towns like I grew up in. Needless to say, going to college at 17 with a 21-year-old roommate from the Valley (South Texas) who had already been to rehab was an eye-opening experience. Despite the fact that I was young and naïve, his hustle spoke to the hustler deep inside of me.

So when he flashed that cash, my eyes bugged out of my head and I immediately asked how he got that money. He simply said he just drove up here. It was an odd statement because he didn't even have a car. As we talked he told me that he drove up from his home in Harlingen, Texas. Harlingen is deep in South Texas near the border of Mexico so heading north you can rest assured that there are vehicle checkpoints looking for drugs. My roommate drove a vehicle carrying marijuana through a checkpoint for $1,500. Well, I don't have a clue to what others would think but I thought . . . can I do it too? My first thought was how can I get some easy money. All I have to do is drive a car? I'm in. That is what you call young and dumb.

I didn't end up making a run through a check point. Instead my roommate came up with another option. We used my financial aid money and brought some steroids and Extacy to sell. We didn't start some low-level drug ring, he was just helping me to flip my money quickly; it was a one-time thing. And you know what, we probably made a few hundred bucks. But whatever money I made, we spent just as quickly. They money vanished because, no matter what amount of money I had, I didn't have the lens to make decisions that lead to a successful tomorrow.

Some of you have just looked for quick money to help you out of a jam but some of you have had to hustle. The thing is that hustlers never sleep. Without an education or marketable skill and that ever important lens of wisdom, the end of one hustle starts the march towards the next. Sadly, hustles tend to skew toward the illegal and continually slide down the morality scale. That also means that some of you might have spent time in jail or prison. If that is the case, I know you have a set of circumstances that all but set you up for failure. Getting a job with a record is something I know nothing about, but this I know: if others have made it, so can you. Just believe God is at work and be diligent in all you do.

How many professional athletes have retired broke? How many bought flashy cars, jewelry, partied, and funded an extravagant lifestyle only to end up with nothing to show for their big contracts? Sure, they tried to invest but none of it worked out because no matter what they tried, the lens with which they viewed those investments was skewed. It is hard to vet an investment when all you have ever known is quick money.

The key thing to take away from a discussion on quick money is this: if you can't get at least two godly men over the age of 45 to give you the green light, listen to them. I'm not talking about taking a calculated risk on a business you want to start. That is another story. I am talking about any venture that offers a quick return on your money. Fast money is a mirage just like consumer debt is a thief. Both look appealing like they will solve a current problem. The reality is that both are an open grave. Run from quick money. Run and don't look back. I only gave you one story of quick money from my life but believe me, it is only by the grace of God that I am not in jail. Not to mention that any of that quick money I made leaked out of my pockets just as quick. It leaked from my pockets because my mind was never looking to tomorrow.

A mind set on today, even the mind that says "Once I get this money it will free me from my past and it will catapult me toward the future" is a mind that has deceived itself. Money is never an answer or a solution. Money is a spiritual matter and only those with wisdom can handle her well. Your money problems are not solved with dollars and cents. Your money problems are solved by how you handle dollars and cents. If you think quick money is the solution then you still are not wise and no matter what debt you cancel, it will manifest in your life again. Birds sing, renters rent, hustlers hustle, and dumb money chases dumb money. Seek wisdom, not a quick buck.

Car Debt

Here is hard pill to swallow for most – borrowing money to buy a car is also one of the most fruitless things in the world. The simple fact is that when you owe money on a car, you are not free to give and not free to follow. You are not free to give at will because every month you have hundreds of dollars in car payments going to a lender. You are not free to follow God because any job move requires that you make enough to cover your payment every month. Instead, if you saved $500 a month for 10 years and get 8% on your money, you would have roughly $92,000 saved up. That is no small amount.

Buying a car with cash and saving for your next car puts you into a position of total freedom, freedom to do anything the kingdom requires. If you want to give that car to someone else, done, here is the title. If a boss fires you because he just doesn't like you, no problem, you don't have a car payment. Not having a car payment most likely means that it will be a while before you can drive the car you really want. It goes back to discipline and delayed gratification. Having a 'nice' car might make you look successful and make you feel good, but by living for today you are borrowing from tomorrow. Before I go further, let me share a failure of mine that helped me learn to absolutely steer clear of auto loan debt.

I was working a sales job that required me to have a truck. I actually prayed for two weeks and sought counsel before buying a new truck. You might say I was doing it right, but wouldn't you know it, about a week after buying it I had the thought: "Why did I buy a *new* truck? I should have gotten something less expensive. Uh?? God, why didn't you let me know before I bought this?" Well fast forward a few months and I left that job and income and couldn't make the payments. My boss owed me $6,000 so I knew that once he paid me I'd be fine. Well, weeks turned into months and he still hadn't paid me. In this particular case, I felt that it was important to let my old boss know that I truly valued God above money, so I told him to not to worry about the money. He could keep it. I firmly believed it wasn't a good witness for me to hound him for money, given my attempts to evangelize at work. So, I decided to do the best thing I could think of and call Nissan and tell them I couldn't pay for the truck and ask them what to do. This was surely better than having them hound me for money I didn't have until they eventually repo' d the truck. So, in what I thought was a moment of godliness, I drove the truck to Nissan and dropped off the keys.

About a week later, I heard a TV preacher talking about a guy who got himself into a similar situation that I was just in weeks before, but he did one thing that never crossed my mind. He called the dealer and asked for another day so he could wash the car, fill the gas tank and get the oil changed because he wanted to return it in the same condition in which he received it. My heart sank. My heart sank because I turned mine in desperately in need of an oil change, badly in need of a wash, and with the gas tank running on fumes. The TV preacher said that God wasn't concerned with the situation you are in but what your heart was like *in* the situation. See, I did make a good decision to call them, but my heart was still focused on money and not the Kingdom. As soon as I knew I was turning in the vehicle, I stopped taking care of it because I didn't want to waste money. I wasn't seeing God as my provider. I felt it was up to me to control what money I had. After all I was doing such a great thing by forgiving a $6,000 debt owed to me. Remember it isn't money you need; it is God's wisdom on handling money.

The point of this story is to remind you that money is spiritual, and you will make mistakes even while trying to honor God. It takes time to grow but none of that story would have happened if I didn't have a car payment. So many of you are crippled by failure. You don't want anyone to see you fail. You are scared of what they might say and think of you. Get over yourself! Once you fail, don't spend your energy covering up your failure, but spend your energy learning not to fail in that area again.

Nobody taught me the value of buying only what you can afford, the deep value of saving, and the weight of debt. Much of my early adult life was just shaped by how I saw the world around me operate. Everybody had a car payment or lease payment. I thought it was just how things worked. Need a car? Go get a loan and get one with a payment you can afford. Simple right? I need something reliable so why not just try and get the best loan rate possible and make my payments on time? At that time, I just didn't have the wisdom to know how to answer those questions. By the way, what did I do without a car you ask? Well, as I was on the phone catching up with my mom, I mentioned that I was going to have to turn in my truck and she simply said, "You can just take mine; God will give me another one." She was able to do that because she didn't have a car payment, I might add. Older and wiser, she saw God as her provider, something I've learned and continue to learn through seeking wisdom.

Let's get some things straight. Most of you are not in a position to pay off your car today and won't be in a position for quite a while. Some of you have a family and are in situations where you owe more than the car is worth. My point is not to tell you that if you have a car payment that you have failed. What I want you to realize is that men should be striving to not owe money, especially on a depreciating mechanical mode of transportation. This is why Christian financial programs are so important. You will need help learning to navigate away from auto loan debt and the sooner you do it, the quicker you will be on your way to handling your money with wisdom. There is not a quick fix, especially for those married, with kids, student loans, and possibly even a mortgage. It can be a long road but if you are single and just starting out, you are able to set yourself up for a success. Follow the narrow path laid out by wisdom.

I am including leasing a car as well in this section. A lease requires a contract and that means you are bound to certain conditions that you can't control. I know that some are reading this and thinking that you just don't know enough about the benefits and conditions that can make leasing better than owning a car outright. But to be honest,

I actually am considering all the benefits. Remember, this is not a numbers game of what is the best way to spend money. This is a discussion on how best to live free from limitations due to the uncertainty of living in a world we can't control. I know the people who leased because it perfectly made monetary sense and then ended up paying $5K to get out of the lease a couple years later. Beyond mileage restrictions, it is the simple fact that once you sign a contract, you are bound to the terms and that contract and it is set up to protect and benefit the leasing company, not you.

Look I know that for most of you, it will be years before you have enough cash on hand to go buy a car outright, let alone a nice car you really want. I've had the car that needed a screwdriver in order to start it. I had another car that I had to push to get it started because the starter went out. When I went on a date with a girl, I parked my heap deep into the empty area of the parking lot so I could ensure I had plenty of runway to push start it. She never had a clue. I eventually traded that car to a dealer because I couldn't afford to fix the clutch. I just rolled my bad debt into another car, another stroke of financial genius. Like I said, I know what is like to not have cash for a car and the feeling of no hope of that changing anytime soon.

Please don't focus on what looks like is an impossible task and instead focus on how you hope to live one day when you are financially free. Michael Jordan didn't become the greatest basketball player in the world in a day. He made the decision to put in the

At some point you have to believe that borrowing money isn't wise.

work on his craft and kept at it for years and the sum of all that time is what produced the greatest basketball in the world. At some point you must begin making decisions that lead you to be able to buy a car with cash. Having money in the bank isn't the point; the point is having ability to live financially free. And not just financially free for yourself but free to help other people. I am sure there are shades of grey like, "What if I can get 0% financing and keep my cash invested so my money can make money?'" and "What if I just borrow and pay it off early?" Those are legitimate questions and that is why there isn't a "Thus sayeth the Lord" at the end of this book. I am not saying it is God's ultimate wisdom to buy a car with cash, but I am saying it is wise to not owe money on a car that you really can't afford because you really haven't learned how to manage money with any real wisdom yet.

Let me leave you with something really practical. I have purchased eight great running cars between $4Kand $8K. From SUV's to small compact cars there are great deals out there. I buy from individuals because there is an automatic discount tied to that type of transaction compared to buying from a dealer. A few years back, you could find good cars on Craigslist and Facebook Marketplace, but dealers and shady people started selling there. They have been overrun with dealers and people trying to flip a car for fast money. Like I said, I like buying from an individual. I like that type of purchase because I can really feel out what type of person they are and ask the question about why they are selling it. Not all dealers are shady, but all dealers are better salesman. And sometime salesmen help themselves by convincing you they are helping you.

Once I was asked by a friend to help them navigate their way as they bought a car from a dealer. The car was picked out and we were in the final step, sitting with the finance person. As he was going through the options, he said that my friend qualified for their 0% interest rate. As he kept talking, I pulled out my calculator and started running the numbers. He was keeping her focused on what her monthly payment could be instead of how much she was actually borrowing. It is a great car sales tactic because us Americans are focused on short term not long term, keeping us focused on what our monthly payments are and not how much we are borrowing and how much we are getting charged for borrowing. Well when he was done, I stopped and asked to get a clarification. "So, to get 0% interest she actually borrows more principle but if she takes the 5% interest rate, she borrows less principle. And if she takes the 5% interest rate there is no penalty for paying it off early right?" My friend already told me they looking to pay off the car early. If she took the 0% interest loan, there would be no benefit of paying it off early. However, she would benefit from the higher interest rate because if she paid it off early, she would actually end up paying less for the vehicle when it was all said and done.

See, the finance guy was not dishonest; he was just looking out for the dealer. If she borrowed more money, what did they care if it is labeled principle or interest? They were looking to make money and if she walked out saying she got 0% financing, she would be happy. Ugh! I hate car dealers. They are not bad; they are just running a business. When you buy from dealer, you are dealing with a company, a business, and when dealing with a business you have to read the fine print. It is just how the world works. Now some like buying from dealers; there isn't a wrong answer. I've done Car Max, Family-Owned Dealers, and Tote the Note lots, so I've just about done it all. I'm just more of a people person when it comes to buying cars, so any chance I can deal with a person who is just looking to sell their own car with no fine print, I take it. I like having the feeling that I believe the person to be honest because of how they answered my questions.

As I write today, the Neighborhood App is where I have found my last two cars I bought. There is just a comfort when you pull up to someone's house and see the car, as opposed to some supermarket parking lot. People that show the car at their house have a real confidence they are not selling some lemon. Who would want an angry buyer that knows where they live? What I look for is a car with 80K-100K miles and that has been taken care of well. I once bought a 10-year-old Acura CL with 66,000 miles. The guy had a log and receipts for every time he bought gas, every oil change, and every service the vehicle had received in the last 10 years. I paid $6,500 hundred for that car and would have paid more if he asked; he took great care of that car. When I sold it, I didn't budge on the price either because I told the potential buyer, "If you can find a car that has been taken care of this well, go get it."

I look for Hondas or Mazdas because I have had great personal experience with them, but the last car I bought was a Kia. It was about 5 years old and only $4,000 with about 60K miles. When I get a car like that, I usually set aside $500 just in case there is something I need to take care of that is unseen. But you would be amazed what people will disclose about a vehicle they own, above a dealer salesman who is just trying to sell a car. Even if he was the most honest guy in the industry, if it wasn't his car, he just doesn't know the car's history. When you have cash, you can take your time and wait for the right car to show up.

Let me leave you with some hope if you don't have $8K laying around. When I bought that Acura, I called my bank and told them I was looking to get a car. At the time, I didn't have great credit, but I had average credit. I told them I was looking for a used car in a certain age range and they told me how much I was approved to borrow. In essence I was a cash buyer because I could shop knowing I could borrow the money from my bank. Once I made the offer and the guy accepted, I called my bank with the VIN number and they overnighted a cashier's check. My next step was to pay that loan off ASAP. I think I paid it off in a year and a half. That is how you buy cash when you don't have the cash. You buy what you can afford and pay it off as soon as earthly possible. The key is to buy a good running car that you can afford.

Right now, if you have a car, it is a used car. Yep, even if you bought it new, it is now a used car. Don't look at used cars as old run-down piles of junk. Just look for a good value. Cars last much longer than they did thirty years ago, and American made cars were not nearly as reliable, but today a Chevy can run as long as a Honda. Take your time, find a car that has been taken care of (someone who has kept records is always best), and try to stay below 100K miles. A good used car could easily last another 100K-150K miles if you take care of it. Just make it your mission to pay cash, and if you have to borrow money, pay off the loan as soon as humanly possible.

Student Loans

The first thing you need to understand about student loans is that you it is a debt of the worst kind. It must be paid no matter what. If debt is evil, student loans are the devil. This may not be something you have never heard before but that doesn't make it less true. Oh sure, somebody out there might tell you that you are investing in yourself but that is a lie. The truth is you are *borrowing money* that you will have to pay back with interest. It is not an investment, it is a loan, plain and simple. I know they sounds like a good idea and you really believe you will have no problem paying them back. After all, you will have plenty of money available once you have that degree, right? Wrong. I am trying to tell you how the world works, not the way you think it works. It isn't like I am some lone voice crying out that student loans are bad. There is a whole segment of people who will testify that student loan debt is a beast they can't tame, not to mention that in the book of Proverbs, God simply states that the borrower is a slave to the lender (Proverbs 22:7). You don't even have to believe in God to know that statement to be true.

Taking longer to graduate so you don't have to borrow money is practicing delayed gratification, and it requires discipline which sets you up for long term success. It all comes down to a simple matter of making mature, informed decisions and having patience. One of the most practical things you can learn as a man is that delayed gratification is how you build anything of worth. Yes, I know that the cost of higher education is the problem and not student loans, but you can't do anything about the cost. You can only control where you get the money and where you go to school. Money comes from work, that is the lens you must look through. I'll cover more about school choice when it comes to education but for now let's stick to student loans.

There isn't one right way to pay for college, but there are options that don't involve borrowing tens of thousands of dollars. For instance, I joined the military to pay off my $45K of student loan debt. Did it suck to live in the army barracks as a 27-year-old until I turned 31? Yes, it did but I also went to grad school and the Army paid for that too. There are so many ways and here is the thing; they all require you to sacrifice time or require you to work more. You are going to get a side hustle. You are going to have to work 50-60 hours during the summer and 20-30 hours during school. You are going to have to find a job that pays better than minimum wage. A job like that just won't provide the income upside needed. Jobs that have commission, great tips, or that provide opportunity for extended hours are needed. You can't think of why it can't be done and instead think of how you are going to make it happen. That is how new paths are forged.

The wide path or easy way is to just borrow money. Student loans are shortcuts, and shortcuts always extract a hefty price. You can try and name all the people you know that borrowed money for school and it worked out okay, but not one of them can say a Bible verse was the foundation for their decision. For every person who would say it is a good path to pay for school, there are countless stories of people that are buried in debt they can't afford. There are organizations that specialize in helping people understand student loans and help them find a way to dig out from under the weight of loans. Many don't know how student loan interest works and how different types of student loans treat interest. You can Google "capitalized interest student loans" to get a quick idea how interest can really make loan repayment more difficult. The Institute of Student Loan Advisers (TISLA) gives free student loan advice and would be a great place to start if you are already in a bad spot.

I would be remiss if I didn't mention that not all who enter college finish college. There is a big downside because after 6 years, 30% of students were not enrolled in college anymore and had not attained a degree,[7] and if you are Black or Hispanic, that percentage is quite higher.[8] That means that if those students borrowed money, they ended up without a degree but still have the burden of paying back student loans. Bankruptcy has helped many restart their financial lives after years of bad financial decisions, but no matter how much debt was wiped away, student loans still remain because they can't be handled with bankruptcy. I just can't stress how much student loans are not your friend. It isn't like you finish with just one loan. The average student graduate with $37,000[9] in loan debt and that can be spread across several loans through various loan programs. And those loans can get sold to third parties making it difficult to track who you owe. Let there be no doubt—these companies are looking to make money and

---

7. http://www.studentclearinghouse.org/nscblog/national-six-year-completion-rate-reaches-highest-level-58-3-percent-since-the-national-student-clearinghouse-research-center-began-tracking/
8. http://www.studentclearinghouse.org/nscblog/national-six-year-completion-rate-reaches-highest-level-58-3-percent-since-the-national-student-clearinghouse-research-center-began-tracking/
9. https://www.debt.org/students/

make things look attractive. Simply telling someone they can have six months with no payments sounds great but when that principle and interest is added back into the loan, you end up paying even more. In a lot of ways, college gives the illusion that you are an adult living in the real world, but college is not the real world and there is no greater example of this than student loans.

Outside of college nobody will ever let you borrow up to hundreds of thousands of dollars with no collateral, no credit check, and no job. Do you think lenders are on your side, looking to help you be the first to graduate in your family? Of course not, they are in business to make money. The outstanding student debt in 2019 was $1.52 trillion. If you assume you will pay it off when you get that great paying job, consider this: $298.9 billion of that outstanding debt is owed by people over age 50, with $67.8 billion owed by those over age 62.[10] Read that again – $67.8 billion still outstanding by those over 62. So much for that high paying job taking care of those loans.

Beyond student loans, avoiding all debt has to be your goal. I highly recommend taking Financial Peace University or Crown Financial. Both of those programs are rooted in a biblical truth. In fact, I just went through Financial Peace just last year and I still found it extremely helpful. The reason I went through it at age 49 was not because I thought it would be new information but because I intentionally wanted to put myself in a position for God to speak to me about how I spend, save, and give away money. I encourage you to "never

10. https://www.credit.com/personal-finance/average-student-loan-debt/

arrive" when it comes to learning about money. As you grow spiritually, your views on money will grow as well. So I say again, if you have not ever taken one of those courses, then I highly recommend you do so.

Let me also be clear that I don't agree with everything in those classes. If you are an entrepreneur, then a lot of those things will not fit for you. The book *Rich Dad Poor Dad* by Robert Kiyosaki might help you. Robert is big on using debt to get cash flow through rental property. Debt financing is a part of a financial model to produce income as opposed to consumer debt, which is just people borrowing to buy something they can't actually afford, like student loans which don't produce anything. A degree is produced by your hard work. Nobody is hired because of a degree; they are hired because an employer thinks you can produce or benefit the company more than another candidate. Someone like Robert Kiyosaki uses debt to produce the income and pay off the property. The point is that God didn't leave a blueprint for everyone to handle money in the same way. Some will always produce more income than others. You need to find out who you are and use money the best way that fits how God made you specifically.

By the way, if you hear me telling you debt is the devil unless you do it this way, then you need to keep reading. When we get to the section on education, we will put student debt into relationship with what a degree produces, and it will shed even more light on student loan debt. My brothers, if you have not entered school or know someone who has not entered college yet, let me be clear that this isn't monopoly money. You will have to repay it and life doesn't stop. Life marches on and trying to manage life is hard enough, especially so if you are buried under school loans. They don't go away with bankruptcy. They will haunt you and you will receive phone calls, emails, and letters that constantly remind you that you must pay. If you are one of the guys who is already under the pressure to repay loans, then I urge you to follow one of the programs I mentioned you earlier. There is freedom but it is found by following wisdom. Follow the guys God put on the planet to help you manage money. You will reap a harvest, and it isn't getting a degree without loans. The harvest is gaining wisdom for yourself.

For many, student loans seem like the only possibility of funding an education. I am sure they would say that they could not have made it without school loans. The truth is that it's all about choices. There are things you *want* to do and things you *need* to do. Borrowing money is always a want, not a need. Once you buy into the idea that student loans are the only way to pay for education then that is exactly what you will do. Oh sure, you are not opposed to working during school, but you just don't see how it can be done without the additional money. But beyond tuition, are you really borrowing money for school or to fund the lifestyle and the dream school you want? If student loans didn't exist would you actually choose another more affordable university? As I said, once you allow debt to enter the equation, you automatically open yourself to high jacking your financial future.

Student loans are an open grave. There is nothing more practical than telling you to avoid student loans at all costs. Some will think I'm going overboard but you can go to

YouTube and search student loan debt and see what comes up. See how many student loan debt success stories you find. I'm not saying they are not out there. I am telling you to run from debt and take a path your father should have laid out for you—**hard work, patience, and delayed gratification**. Paying for college in today's world is expensive. Borrowing money to pay for it seem logical and, for most people, the only way to pay for it. But wisdom is above logic. You want to be a man free to make his own decisions? Remember avoid student loan debt at all costs. If you borrow to pay for school, you will be a slave to that debt and will never be free to give as you wish.

Buying A Home

Being a veteran, I had the luxury of using a no cash down VA Loan, but most people will have to have a large sum of money for a down payment. Buying a house is a great way to create wealth but many home buyers really need to educate themselves before buying. I should rephrase that: first time home buyers need to learn from an older, wiser believer before buying a home. In fact, years before buying a house (I'd say as early as 18) you need to start figuring out what you need and start making an intentional plan. Remember, goals without plans are just wishes. There are so many different paths to home ownership and so many different variables, like income, existing debt, credit rating, being married or single, where you live, job stability, and on and on, and most importantly where you are in your current understanding of how money works in the Kingdom of God.

As you consider this section, I want to you to be see yourself as a homeowners as soon as possible. For someone young it may seem like that is decades away, but I can promise you that it is closer than you think, especially if you plan early. For others (in their 30's and currently living out the consequences of their mistakes, for example), I can only try to convince you that you are still very young. You might feel like you have blown it, but I can assure you that with your mind set on God and giving, not money, you are closer than you think. I spent my entire 30's making up for the mistakes of my 20's. Those credit card companies offering free T-shirts on campus for applying for a credit card and those easy application department credit cards were just too alluring for me. I could get something big … and only pay $15 a month? Hey, I can pay $15 a month, so why not? I got caught in the credit card net along with hundreds of thousands of college student around the country.

At 39 years old I returned home from my honeymoon and moved into the house my wife owned and carrying my possessions in black trash bags. You might think it sounds sad but the back story is that I got rid of any furniture I accumulated before spending 15 months working in Iraq as a civilian on a military base in hopes of finally getting rid of all bad debt. When I came back at age 36, I was totally debt free and free to give anytime, anywhere to anyone and finally ready to live financially free. Of course, it took another 7 years before that truck repo was removed from my credit, so it wasn't until age 43 that my credit score improved. Once again, the reason I share that with you is so that, first and foremost you learn to avoid dumb mistakes and you know that it is never too late to change. I might have been a 39-year-old man with no real possessions, but I was financially free. Trust me, being free is better than being bound up in debt but having many possessions.

I have heard it said that most people overestimate what they can do in a year and underestimate what they can do in twenty years. It is so true. Change takes time, thus embrace the process and you will go farther than you ever imagined. The key will be you embracing wisdom wherever you can get it.

So here it comes—buying a house is a spiritual decision as well. Think about it: Adam being placed in the garden—spiritual. Abraham called to a land—spiritual. Joseph sold off to Egypt—spiritual. Hebrews leaving Egypt—spiritual, and on and on throughout the Old Testament. In the New Testament Jesus and His disciples only travel to where God wants them. Paul says the Holy Spirit told him where to go and would not let him go other places. Now moving without God's leading isn't evil or a sin, but if you want to follow God as closely as possible, you have to let God be the driving force in a geographical move. That is done by inviting God into the process and not just in prayer but in seeking counsel.

Buying a home means you will be moving and moving is always spiritual.

I have a friend that is a realtor and that it exactly how he advises his clients. He asks why they are moving and even challenges them if their move takes them away from deep church relationships just so they can get a bigger, better house.

He isn't telling them they are wrong, but he is telling them to consider their spiritual health above material possessions. Just follow the history of God people. A move is always led by God, even when disciplining them. He *moved* them out of the land. I am His temple, my home is the tabernacle, if you will. My home is where I worship, pray, lay down my life for my wife. My home should be set apart for the Lord and not just a space that fits my family's needs. I should move when He moves me. Let me tell you about another failure, specifically my most recent move.

We had moved for ministry and rented until we found out where we wanted to live in the city of Houston. During that time, we switched from W-2 income to self-income, so we had to wait three years before buying a house. Tired of renting a house with nasty carpets, incredibly high electric bills, roof rat battles, slug trails on the carpet, an occasional mouse, and other first world inconveniences, we just looked at the map and asked, "Where can we get the most house for the amount we are pre-approved for?" It was not wrong, it just wasn't spiritual. Our previous moves were led by God, but this one . . . I just took my eye off the ball.

But back to the practical. This is the third house my wife and I have owned, the second we bought together. All of them have been a 30-year fixed mortgage. That is pretty much the standard way people buy a home. But why is 30 years what we all choose? Why not get pay it off earlier? Yes, there are techniques to pay it off earlier but why not use a 20-year mortgage or a 15-year mortgage? Simple, because we just don't think that way. Instead, we all tend to follow the way the world around us operates. If you get a 15-year mortgage, you might have to buy less house, but you would be out of debt sooner and isn't that better? I wish my Christian brothers and sisters in the mortgage loan business would sit down with us and help us think spiritually. I have never had someone stop and say to me, "Hey, I know you are trying to be a good follower of Jesus. Have you ever considered doing a shorter mortgage term? You might have to buy a less expensive house, but you would be out of debt sooner and that could really help you give." Once again, it isn't wrong to do a 30-year mortgage, but I contend that 99% of us just don't live intentionally enough with how we buy; we have goals but not enough plans. Once again, wisdom will come as you learn from others, which means you will have to ask for help. And don't just ask for help, ask for help from those that have experience in that particular area and ask them why their way is the best and how it benefits the Kingdom. Learning why will help you teach someone else down the line.

Some things may not benefit the Kingdom but they sure will help you. For instance, don't buy a house that faces east if you live in the south. If you do, you won't be able to enjoy your backyard because of the heat from the setting sun, not to mention what the sun will do to your stained front door. If you have kids, don't fall in love with a house and ignore a small backyard; you will regret it. If you have a large family, consider acoustics and maybe value homes with two living spaces. And by all means, learn about what it takes to maintain a home, like fixing clogged sinks and toilets, HVAC maintenance, yard maintenance costs, and others little things that are just part of owning the home. There are all kinds of non-kingdom tips that you can pick up from friends and as you do, ask what mistakes they made. You are just going to have to be intentional about your life; always asking how and why from those older than you.

Follow the advice of Financial Peace University, Crown Financial, or some other organization regarding how to pay off your house as soon as possible. You also must consider how owning a house could end up paying you money each month. Remember that friend of mine who bought a house when he didn't even have a job? Well, 15 years later that house is still paying him rent every month. That, my friends, is how your money works for you. Oh, and by the way, lest you think he was just chasing money, he was also one of the guys who let me live rent free when God was disciplining me. And for you young guys, consider his example carefully.

I had a friend in college who owned a condo while in college. He rented out the other rooms and that paid his mortgage. Instead of paying rent, he bought a house and built wealth. Once again, I knew about it and I thought about what a great idea it was and how I would love to be in a place where I can help my kids do that. I saw it and believed I could do it sometime in the future, not knowing I was just as capable. I just didn't have lens for that life. If you are reading this, chances are that is how you think. . . . "Someday, I'll do it."

I'm telling you, owning a home is closer than you think. How many of you have sat down with a mortgage guy and asked how far away you are and what you need to do? Make the call. When you are single and own a home, you can do it for financial reasons or even for ministry

You must have a plan or all you have is a big fat wish.

reasons. I have a friend who owned his home and he always had guys living in his house, but he rarely charged rent. He used his house as a place to accomplish ministry. And when he got married, he and his wife continued to use the house the same way. You can do it, but it can't just be a goal.

Buying a home is wise but buying a home that will increase in value and not financially burden you is even wiser. "You make your money on the buy" and "Location, location, location" are common real estate phrases that I agree with. However, in order to profit from buying a house, you need to think spiritually. You need to allow God to guide you as best you can. Good, better, and best are typically how our decisions play out in life. There definitely are some right and wrong decisions, but mostly we make decisions that could have been better. God has not obligated Himself to come to you in a dream and tell you to buy a specific house and pay a specific amount. He isn't your genie. He has made wise counsel available to you. Buy a home to help others, increase wealth, generate income, provide a place for your family to live. . . . Whatever you do, don't think that home ownership is only for others. It is for *you* and if *you* sacrifice, it will be sooner rather than later.

So what is the practical wisdom here? You need to get with someone who knows how the industry works and find out what you need to do to buy a house. Having an owner mentality is different from a renter's mentality. Renter's typically don't consider long term costs of their decisions. **Men need to think beyond today.** When you grow up without a father, it can be tough to cultivate a long-term mentality. If you are married, leading your wife means actually leading.

You can't say you want to buy her a house but not show her *how* you are leading her into it. Men need to be humble and there is nothing more humbling than asking for help.

Of course there are people for whom homeownership doesn't work. Maybe you're in the military or oil industry and get moved every couple of years. Maybe you did some research and found that considering the things you value, renting is actually a better decision for you. Whatever your reasoning, I desire you to have a long-term outlook on life and plant roots in a community.

For the believer, even homeownership is more than just creating wealth and stability. It allows you to be a part of a community. When you own the home, you care about who is on your city council, who lives on your street, what the school district votes on. When you invest in the community, you care about it and seek its well-being. The more you care about the community, the more you engage people with the Kingdom.

Saving

Looking back, it is easy to identify the story that really should have taught me the value of having a savings. My graduating semester of college I worked in Dallas, lived about 20 minutes north of Dallas and went to University of North Texas another 20 min north of where I lived. My problem is that I blew the engine on my car and needed $1,500 to get it fixed. That means I needed to work to pay for the car, but I needed the car to get to school so I could finish my degree and get home to sleep; classic catch 22. The mechanic happened to be the best guy in that field ever and fixed my car and let me pay out the repairs in a couple of months. But for a good while, I was catching rides where I could, living on couches, and finding any way possible to get to class.

See, for me in college it was much cheaper to spend $1.50 on a cheap quart of oil rather than spend $30 on an oil change. My tires were always bald and general maintenance was always trumped by whatever other short-term priorities I had in that moment. I can't think of a time when I ever had savings. I'm not talking the first couple of weeks after getting my Pell grant, but having some money set aside for a rainy day. I know you are not an idiot and realize that you are supposed to change your oil. The key point is to fully embrace that however inconvenient it may be, maintenance is cheap, fixing broken things is expensive. The bill always comes due.

There are a couple of reasons many of my fatherless brothers are or were in that same boat I was. One reason is because there is no tomorrow. Why would you save money when your whole life, today is all you are trying to get through? The other reason you don't or didn't save is because you thought you didn't have any money to save. The truth is that you didn't value tomorrow enough to take care of your future self.

For the first set of guys, I get it, truly I do. You can't afford to save when you barely have enough for today. The truth is that you have a poverty mentality. It is simply that you don't live as if God is really your provider. Instead, you live as if you are an orphan without help from a loving father. To the non-believer you may think in terms of what you don't have instead of what it would take to have what you need, then taking the steps to get there. Now it isn't your fault necessarily. Typically, life has taught you that you are poor and the rich have someone helping them out; the rich can afford to save. After all, Jesus said you will always have poor among you, right?

One of the guys I have learned from tremendously is a guy named Rabbi Daniel Lapin. He wrote a book called *Thou Shall Prosper* that really helped me understand money in a new light. I am not sure it was in that book or one of his podcasts, either way he said something very profound: God said that there would always be poor, but understanding the Hebrew text is important and adds clarity. They were not to think of themselves as poor. When you think of yourselves as poor, you look for someone to help you out. But if you never consider yourselves as poor then you can see there is always someone with less that *you* can help. This also help you strive to have more like those you see that have more than you currently do.

The key is to understand that even if you are poor, you always have what you need to give. I've seen the family who hit hard times, received help from the state's food program for a while but still helped someone out who had less by buying them groceries. It isn't an increase in money that helps you get out of poverty. It is the change of lens that helps you still be a giver and trust God with your needs. My mom lived on Social Security alone and still gave me a car knowing that God would take care of her. God was her provider and she was not financially bound by her monthly Social Security check.

I have mentioned it a couple of times and I will expand more on it later, but you have to notice how I mentioned giving alongside with not having money. When you don't have money, you typically won't save and giving seems counter-intuitive. The crazy thing is that I have found that those that give sacrificially are typically those who have less or have a rough past of not having much. Once you have been without, you know how hard it is and you jump at the chance to help someone when you can. But saving is almost never an option for someone with little; they just can't afford it.

But my dear brothers, saving is always possible. God doesn't say, "Consider the ant" to only those who have money (Proverbs 6:6-11). Savings takes discipline, trust, and a new lens of life. In Financial Peace University, David Ramsey breaks things down into baby steps. The first baby step is saving $1,000. For some that is just moving funds via online banking but for others it requires a year of sacrificing. Back in college I could have benefitted from saving $1,000, but I just didn't think past the moment. You have to follow the wisdom of guys like Dave Ramsey, Larry Burkett, Randy Alcorn, Rabbi Lapin, or anyone gifted by God to help his people learn to handle money with a Kingdom lens.

Savings and investing, which we will cover next, are not about money. They are about serving others. When God rescued His people from bondage in Egypt, it wasn't just to free them. He didn't say, "Let my people go PERIOD." Moses and Aaron told Pharaoh that God said, "Let me people go *so that they might worship me.*" God doesn't remove you from a situation for the sake of freeing you but so that you might serve Him. You save and invest, not in an attempt to be free from poverty but so that you might be free to serve God. He has to be the director of it all.

When my wife and I left Dallas to help plant a church in Houston, I would say that I fully trusted God financially. In fact, I would say I would have felt 100% comfortable answering that question with a polygraph testing me. When we sold our house in Dallas, we made money and set that aside for the purchase of a new house once we figured out where He would have us lay down roots. If you know anything about church planting, then you know that first couple of years can be financially difficult. At that time, we were just a family of four, but our salary was only $1,000 per month. Well, our rent alone was $1,250 so each month was an exercise of faith. We knew that our church stipend would increase sometime and we had a little income from other areas, so we just trusted God. As the months went by, we started dipping into that money meant for a new house. We didn't complain but our prayers were, "Hey God, don't know if you have noticed but we are spending that money for our next house." That went on for a while and every now and then someone would hand us a check mentioning they felt God wanted them to give to us. Now we were never in dire straits but slowly we came to understand that *we* were the ones that labeled that money as new house savings. God, on the other hand, labeled that money as provision. That money was provision for us during that time and without our mind focused on God, we felt nervous.

Savings isn't meant to give us a sense of security but to be a vehicle for God to minister to us and those around us in times of need. Save so that you might fix your broken car but also so that you might fix your neighbors' car. The only way to live like that is to live as if God is your provider. It will free you up to save nickel by nickel or by only living on a percentage of your paycheck. The only right way is to do so in hopes of serving God with savings.

If you have that poverty mentality and believe you can't afford to save, how do you begin? Simply set small goals, make a plan, stay disciplined, and trust God. If you have child support, an hourly job, a wife, and rent and there just isn't anything left, how do you save? Simply set small goals, stay disciplined, and trust God. That means you are going to have to give up that Coke, candy, treat, or whatever extra, sell something online just so you can have something to save, or cut somebody's yard to make a little extra. Saving is all about not spending today so you can have something tomorrow. It is trusting that God will provide what you need today, not necessarily what you want. Those wants are going to have to be put on hold. The truth is that you can't afford to NOT save.

My practical advice here is to really engage with God and ask Him how you can save, especially when your monthly bills are beyond your monthly income. God is a multiplier of five loaves and a jar of oil (John 6:1-14; 2 Kings 4:1-7) and He can make a way. Those financial courses give great wisdom, but it will only be the Spirit of God that will provoke change and move you from faith to action. There is great joy in giving but there is also great joy in receiving when you know it is God's provision. For some of you, before you will ever be able to save enough to help someone else, it will be you with the need. Don't be afraid to ask for help. There are brothers and sisters that would love to help. Pride can keep you from asking sometimes or even our faith that leads us to believe that God will provide for us miraculously. Pride is defeated by humility. And that belief that God will provide a miracle is checked with the biblical understanding that God's typical mode of helping people is through other people (2 Corinthians 1:3-4; Ephesians 4:28). Just remember that saving isn't about having money, it is about being wise with money for the sake of the Kingdom.

Investing

If there is one thing I lament at this stage in my life is the amount of money I have to invest. By investment I mean it is wonderful when your money is making money. You invest with disposable income (extra money), not with your rent money. That is why school loans are not an investment because it isn't extra money. School loans are meant to pay for food, rent, books, tuition, gas, and utilities during school.

Now concerning investing, the main term you might have heard before is compound interest. Basically, when the interest you earn on an investment gets reinvested, it is created a snowball effect that dramatically increases the value of your investment over time.

I can remember as far back as high school of the textbook example of two guys who invested money at different times of their lives. Let's say you and a friend Steve are the same age. At 20 you invested $100 a month for 10 years and then stopped investing. Your buddy Steve waited until age 30 before he began investing. Steve started investing $100 a month for the next 30 years. (Assuming you both earned 7% interest compounded monthly.) Well even though you only invested for 10 years and stopped putting in money, your money never stopped working for you. You only put in $12,000 over 10 years but that money grew to $141,303. Meanwhile, Steve put in $36,000 and ended up with $122,708. So even though you put in $24,000 less than Steve, because you started 10 years earlier, the power of compound interest made your money grow beyond his. The lesson: the earlier you can live with a long-term lens when it comes to money, the more the future version of yourself will thank you.

Oh, how I wish I embraced that lesson earlier. But like saving, I just couldn't see well enough to live like that. Of course, investing is not a plug and crank, one size fit all financial product so going into all the options just isn't possible. You can flip houses, buy rental properties, invest in mutual funds, fund your 401k to the max, and on and on and on. Investing really is a function of time and appreciation of some sort of asset(s). Investing looks to fund the future you. Genesis 49:27 says, "Benjamin is a ravenous wolf, in the morning devouring the prey and at evening dividing the spoil." Investing is devouring the prey now so you can have something to divide in the evening. There is a future you that will need to eat. That future you may not be in good health. That future you may be able to work anymore. It is up to the young you, the guy in the mirror today, to go out and devour they prey so you can divide the spoils with future you. Investing requires you to be a shrewd and calculated so that your money makes money, freeing you up to do something else. It is really about giving you the freedom to do those things you want to do, when you want to do them without worrying about having to earn today's food.

At some point, what you bring to the table at work will diminish in the eyes of an employer. They will be looking to get younger at that position, lessen salaries, get more productivity, and acquire new ideas. Sooner or later a company will no longer require your services and other companies won't have a place for you. In those days, you will still need to have money to live and give. As soon as you have disposable income, you must find someone to help you invest. Some of you have skillsets that make investing easy because you see opportunity, and others need to rely on someone to handle things for you. There is no best way, but the goal is the same: getting as much return on your investment as possible in the time that you have to earn money.

You may be at many life stages—young and single, married, divorced, parents, saddled with debt, or debt free. It is all about you learning to have a lens that looks toward the future but never turns a blind eye to those in need. How we choose to invest (401k, Roth IRA, renting houses, flipping houses . . .) are labels we use to help us plan, but those labels have to be written in pencil. God is the one who directs our hearts. I have a friend who dipped into his retirement account to buy someone a car. That is a bad financial decision for many reasons, but it was the best Kingdom decision because he took care of someone's immediate needs. You must fight to not let money in any form become an idol. God is your provider. You won't take anything with you and the generations behind you will be blessed by shrewd investing. Just don't lie to yourself and think that if you don't have enough in a retirement account that you are a failure. Faithfulness is the only measurement God uses in any area of our lives. Be faithful to be the best believer you can.

You men are all different so there is no lone voice to listen to for investment ideas or ways to make money. David Ramsey has some good thoughts but so does Grant Cardone, Warren Buffet, David Tepper, or Gary Vaynerchuk. There are countless books that you could read like *The Intelligent Investor* by Benjamin Graham *or Think and Grow Rich* by Napoleon Hill, but you can't let the options paralyze you. Looking forward with a good heart is the first step, but keep your eyes and ears open because God is always steps ahead of you. He knows your talents, shortcomings, desires, degree of faith, and every thought tucked in the corners of your mind. As you discover more of who you are at the deepest levels of your soul, just remember to think investment. Invest in people as a priority but financial investment will feed that old man you will see in the mirror down the line.

The one thing I don't want you to hear when I say investment is the word retirement. The simple reason is that I don't believe in retirement. I am not saying you should have a job until the day you die. I just want to be clear that I don't believe you should work, save, and invest so that one day you can sit by the pool, go on trips, and finally do all the things you want to do without worrying about money. This idea of retirement is born out of the 1950's when retirement communities began advertising and influencing people toward selfishness, telling them that, now that their work was done, all they needed to worry about was their own enjoyment. . The prescription became 'work is done now, just worry about your enjoyment'. I believe retirement means that you don't need to work anymore in order to provide for your daily needs and even if you can't physically work as before, you find ways to be a productive member of society for the benefit of all. Just like when you were young, you enjoyed what you had, paid your own expenses, gave to others, and funded daily expenses with your job. When you get older, you will enjoy what you have, pay your own expenses, but fund it with what you saved and invested. You will always be happier in life when you able to help others. Invest but invest knowing that you are putting money aside to give to the future you and to help someone else in the future. Invest to so you can continue to give in the future, and you will find that you'll have more than if you just invested for yourself. To divide the spoil in the future, you must slay some beasts today.

Giving

Giving is the most important part of handling money wisely. To be the answer to someone else's prayer is to be the hands of God at the most basic level. I have always said that givers give, plain and simple. For some, giving is natural but for others it might take some time to become a cheerful giver. I was once asked by a pastor to look in on a couple to see what needs they might have. The husband was recently hospitalized, so I visited them and discovered that travel and gas prices were creating a real problem for them. At the time I was in a men's small group at our church. It was up to about 20 guys meeting for Bible study and mutual encouragement. In that meeting I shared the need and assumed they would jump at the chance to help out. Most of the guys had good paying jobs and plenty of disposable income. Sadly, I collected $15 from that entire group. As I was about to leave one of the guys asked me if I still needed money. He pulled out a good roll of money and peeled off a $5 bill. It was so nonchalant that it seemed totally disingenuous. I felt ashamed of my group of friends, a Bible study group of friends no less. It turned out okay, but if it wasn't for a good understanding of giving, I would have been bitter.

In Philippians 4:10-18, the Apostle Paul says:

> *I rejoiced in the Lord greatly that now at length you have revived your concern for me. You were indeed concerned for me, but you had no opportunity. Not that I am speaking of being in need, for I have learned in whatever situation I am to be content. I know how to be brought low, and I know how to abound. In any and every circumstance, I have learned the secret of facing plenty and hunger, abundance and need. I can do all things through him who strengthens me.*
>
> *Yet it was kind of you to share my trouble. And you Philippians yourselves know that in the beginning of the gospel, when I left Macedonia, no church entered into partnership with me in giving and receiving, except you only. Even in Thessalonica you sent me help for my needs once and again. Not that I seek the gift, but I seek the fruit that increases to your credit. I have received full payment, and more. I am well supplied, having received from Epaphroditus the gifts you sent, a fragrant offering, a sacrifice acceptable and pleasing to God.*

One of the things I learned from this passage was how Paul sees giving. He was happy for the giver of the gift. He sought the fruit that reveals a changed heart. Their sacrifice was a fragrant offering to God. See Paul, knew God would provide for him so he was not worried about where it would come from or when. He cared about people, not things. The giver or the one who provided for his needs was someone who was giving to God and that made him happy. So when my men's group didn't help provide the needs of that couple dealing with medical and travel issues, it was sad because they missed the opportunity to help someone else. I couldn't be bitter because they still needed growth to happen in their hearts. It didn't make me better than them, it just meant I was placed there to help them in this area as they were there to help me in my areas of weakness.

When giving, you have to see it as an opportunity to be a part of God's provision. What could be better than to trust God with your needs and give to provide someone else's needs? And when you are the one receiving, you can actually be happy for the giver and let them know their gift is a wonderful fragrance to God. Giving is crucial to practical manhood. Seek to give and to give cheerfully. In the entire Bible there is only one reference to the *type* of person that God loves. In 2 Corinthians 9:7, it says God loves a cheerful giver. I don't want to convince you to give; I invite you to give, give, give.

There isn't a specific way to give, it is always about the heart.

Some love to give to people, others like to give to non-profits. Some feel like great stewards if their gift is tax deductible and others like to give entirely in secret. My best thought would be to encourage you to do some personal bible study and whatever you do, do it in faith. A book I found helpful can be downloaded for free. It is called *A Guide To New Testament Giving*[11] by Jim McClarty. My hope is that you always give from a cheerful heart regardless of what you call it. Taking care of people is always about the heart and thus, I hope you give to them cheerfully. The more cheerfully you give, you will find that both today and tomorrow's provision is already taken care of by God, and as a result, money transforms from a security blanket to just a tool in your toolbox.

Life After Death

Even after death, life will go on for your loved ones. I can't cover money without talking about leaving your family with financial assistance to handle final expenses and beyond. During wedding planning, as your fiancé is deep in wedding details, you should be chatting with a lawyer to get your will and accompanying documents together. This will be the very first thing you will do to show care and concern for your wife. If you are married with no children, it should be straight forward. The only real decision is how much life insurance to get for each of you. I'd suggest a simple 20 or 30-year term life insurance policy, and asking around for an independent insurance representative will set the wheels in motion. As soon as kids come into the picture, you'll need to update everything.

---

11. http://salvationbygrace.org/wp-content/uploads/2014/12/grace_giving.pdf

Now, if you are currently married and have kids, my greatest hope is that you have a will and life insurance in place. If you don't, put this book down and find a lawyer to create your wills. A will and life insurance policies are put into place relatively quickly and there are endless ways to set things up. A typical will should only cost around $400. The way I set mine up isn't the only way, but I think I should share some details and give some explanations to give you some insight.

My wife and I both have a life insurance policy where the other is the beneficiary, but I also have an additional policy that has a trust named as the beneficiary. The reasoning is that if I die, I am not sure how my wife would react. I'm not suggesting she might snap and spend all the money on Snickers bars and handbags. But with five kids, it could be easy to go through a death benefit relatively quickly, especially during times of heavy emotional stress. Thus, the second policy is intended to take care of the kids in case that money runs out, there is an unexpected need, or to provide for them when they grow up. A guy I trust is the trustee of that money so if she needed to access it, she would ask him and he could release any funds she needs. That is also a safeguard in case she remarries and her new husband isn't that great with money; he can't spend the kid's money. Now, my friend the trustee can't spend the money, he can only manage it on my kid's behalf. So if I die, my wife would have a pretty good sum that she controls and there is a second sum that is intended to only benefit the kids if need arises. Then when each kid turns 18, they get a third of their share. They get their next third at 25 and their final third at 35.

I split their distributions because this isn't intended to be some windfall. It safeguards them from making dumb decisions that a typical 18 years old make. Then at 25, after they finish college, they get a chunk to help them get a house or pay off bad debts. And then the final third should be a blessing as they have their own families.

The other key component will be who gets your kids in the event both of you die. This can be an interesting conversation if both of you have family members that are not stable. I don't have a suggestion other than to encourage you to look out for the interest of your children. By the way, this is another reason I have that second insurance policy that funds a trust. I want to ensure the person who gets our kids get money to take care of them, but I also want to protect my kids' future.

Why so much emphasis on who gets money? Why not give it all to my wife? I have been around several families where the husband suddenly passed, and every wife reacted differently. But one thing is common to all of them; their husband's memory is found everywhere. Everybody makes changes, gets away, or wants to escape in some way. It is the scale that can cause money to flow and shorten the lifespan of that death benefit. Take my mom for instance; she was floored by the loss of my dad. She received life insurance and a settlement from the trucking company responsible for my father's death. Those first couple of years we had it made. We took trips, got a new car, helped out other family members, and some people even took advantage of my mom. It didn't take long for that money to run dry and for us to be a struggling family in a small town for the majority of my life.

One of my bosses at the financial planning firm I worked for had a client whose husband passed and received a sizeable death benefit. When he went to check on her, she had just bought an RV (they are not cheap) and was planning on taking the kids on a long trip for the summer. Another widow moved across the country to a city she had no connections to and bought a five bedroom, half million-dollar house for her two toddler daughters and all the new furniture to go with it. Now that doesn't mean your wife will go beyond painting a few rooms. And I certainly am not throwing stones at any of these women. They just experienced a gut wrenching, life altering event and it is completely understandable they made those decisions. But I want you to ask around, talk with your wife, and come up with a plan that sets you up for success because none of us know how we would respond. That is why you make decisions before emotions cloud your judgment. Just keep in mind that if you are married, getting your house in order is not only a good thing, but also an absolute necessity. As a single person, it would be nice to just have a small policy to pay for final expenses and maybe bless siblings. Just be intentional, not controlling.

The reason is simple; it is one last action of loving your family. Following the funeral and everyone is gone, there is the silence in the house that becomes so loud she just can't help missing the sound of you in the house. Imagine your wife going into your closet and taking a shirt you wore. She draws it in close to just remember your scent. There alone in a closet with only the memory of you, do you really want her to be snapped back to reality wondering if she has to money cover the mortgage or rent? Give them some time to grieve, get back on their feet, and try to start over without worrying about finances. Even if you are in a bad financial spot currently, a small life insurance policy will only take a small sacrifice. There is nothing more practical in manhood that loving your spouse and family by providing something if you are gone.

At some point, you will die and the world will go on. You can pass one more lesson to your kids and you can love your wife one last time by simply making sure they don't suffer financially as they mourn your loss. As I mentioned, there are so many ways to set up a will and the accompanying documents, but don't wait. My father was just going to a job interview, my uncle was just driving from work, my sister-in-law was asleep in bed and all of them thought they would wake up another day. This isn't about fear of death, it is simply understanding that I am not God and my life is just a vapor. The best I can do is fear God, obey him, enjoy my life, and love people.

Credit Cards

This will be the shortest section under the banner of money. First hear this loud and clear, you should not use a credit card unless you can pay off the balance each month and have the discipline to do so without fail. The simple reason is because is if you keep a balance, you practice living in debt and that is a bad habit and some people might say that you should not have a credit card. Dave Ramsey, whom I believe to be much more capable in helping people live debt free than I, is one of those people. But like I said, I don't agree with everything he says, and I have two good reasons. First, if you can manage it well, it helps build good credit and, like it or not, good credit matters in this physical world. Good credit effects what you pay in car insurance, in buying a house and it opens the door if you want to run your own business. The other reason is because of what a credit card protects. A credit card protects *your* money. If you make your purchases with a debit card, you are putting your money in jeopardy. Identity theft and theft of banking information are billion dollars issues in the world. If someone steals your banking card info, you should be able to get your money back, but it will take a long while and it causes some real problems, especially when you are living paycheck to paycheck. If you use a credit card, you are not using your money but the credit card company's money, and according to the Federal Credit Billing Act, you are not liable for fraudulent charges. Simply dispute them, and you will have a new card sent out to you in a couple of days and all your money is safe, sitting in your bank. But every time you swipe a debit card, your personal banking information is out in the open.

With that said, I must repeat, if you can't pay off the balance each month, have nothing to do with credit cards. Credit cards are a pitfall and getting out from under them is a beast. On college campuses around the country there are companies itching for you to apply for a credit card. Absolutely none of these companies are on your side. Their greatest desire is for you to charge and maintain a high balance so they can charge interest. Thinking you can get that thing you want for only $15 a month is a trap. A credit card is only useful to the extent it serves your wise purposes. The only way this happens is with discipline and wisdom.

Don't want to live a life paying off debt? The solution is simple—don't amass consumer debt. It is easier to *stay* out of consumer debt than it is to *get out* of consumer debt. It is all about the lens with which you see through. If you see a credit card as a means of helping you out until you can catch up, you have already lost. It is just a matter of time until life events take a turn and you use the credit card to pay for something that you don't really have the funds to pay for. The next thing you know, you are making a minimum monthly payment because you didn't get enough hours at work. You may tell yourself that next month you'll make it up and pay it off, but soon you will wake up and you are in thousands of dollars of credit card debt. A credit card is not a savior to help you in a time of need. That position is filled by God. A credit card is only a tool. You can use it wisely or you will fall prey to the consumer credit card monster. Once again, I have been there brother, and I plead with you, do not ever carry a balance. If you can't easily pay it off monthly, then don't use it.

For some of you the only way to get back into the credit card game is through a secured credit card. Sorry brothers, it is what it is. I've been there, too. Just make a plan and work that plan. I had to take $300 and send it to a credit card company so they would give me a credit card with a $300 limit. That was in my early thirties, so I am not sitting here telling you tales from the mountaintop. I am telling you what it is like at the bottom and how to start climbing out of the hole you dug for yourself. It takes a lot of work and disciplined decisions to get the stench of past failures off your life.

Beyond pushing you to people you know that run their finances well, there is also a site called Nerdwallet.com that is a great resource in helping you find a card that fits your needs. As I mentioned earlier, some would say to cut up every single last of your credit cards and I won't say they are wrong. What I will say is that there is no one size fits all system so I can't tell you which say to go. You are going to have to man up, ask around, and embrace the fact that no man is your judge. If you do that, you will be on your way to learning wisdom, and wisdom will take you places you never thought possible.

Insurance

In today's world there are so many types of insurance products and so many ways to approach them. Instead of going through all of them, I believe it would be most helpful to help you understand insurance as a whole. Regardless of the type of insurance product, all insurance works the same way. There are three components: the premium, the payout, and the contract. The premium is the amount you pay, the payout is the amount the insurance company will pay you, and the contract is the wording that says under what conditions they will pay. The key thing to understand is that of the three you only get to pick two. If you want to get paid the most benefit and get the best wording, the insurance company is going to determine the premium. If you want the lowest premium and the best wording, the insurance company will get to pick the payout. You can't have your cake and eat it too.

With insurance you are betting something negative happens and they are betting it does not happen. All an insurance company really does is use statistics to give them the probability of certain events happening. Then they get enough people to pay a premium that will cover over and above any payouts they would have to make. To be honest, you don't need to know too much about insurance, you really just need to connect with an independent insurance person to help walk you through your needs. There is not a one size fits all solution and certain stages of life will dictate certain needs. You just need to be aware that beyond the government's requirements for things like auto insurance, you should look for areas where you are economically exposed and then put together a plan. It isn't the plan that will save you, it is that you are thinking like a man and considering how to attack life and not just react.

Thus, I can't tell you what is right for you. My hope is to lead you to the water and hope you drink. You'll have to wade the waters yourself and consider health insurance, life insurance, long term disability insurance, disability insurance, auto insurance, homeowners' insurance, home warranties, renters' insurance, dental insurance, etc. These require you thinking through and actively choosing to have insurance or not to have it. I don't have dental insurance because I can pay for that out of pocket, but there was a time when I did have it because the cost was cheap, and it provided me with what I needed. I don't have disability insurance but if I worked construction or any job where my income would be totally lost overnight if something happened to me physically, you can bet that I would have disability insurance, especially if I had a family.

It is the age of information and social media. Make one post asking if someone knows anyone who can help you look for different types of insurance and you will get multiple responses. After having someone look at your insurance needs, don't assume what they say is the gospel. You should have someone else give you another set of eyes on your life and let them give their thoughts as well. You don't want to be sold something, but to be informed and then buy only what you need. The difference between being 'sold' and you 'buying' is that a seller is only looking out for their needs. Someone who will inform you and let you pick what you buy is probably someone who is in it for the long-term relationship.

As a business owner, I can tell you that word of mouth is the absolute best advertising. Someone who people rave about is better to do business with than someone who is just cheaper. Cost is never as important as value. Insurance is about value. Am I getting the best possible benefit for what I am paying? That is value. You want to protect yourself with insurance, but you can't protect your life from life's events. You just want to minimize your downside.

Always remember that you can't buy life insurance. I'm not talking about insurance in case you die, I am saying that life is coming for us all and we can't be 100% protected. You could have a great health insurance policy, and yet your child could become sick and your insurance company could say it is not covered. It happens every day across every socio-economic level. Insurance companies are in business to make money and if denying your claim fits their needs, they will make a payout impossible.

We use a health sharing plan called Samaritan Ministries but there are others like Medi-Share. I like it because every month I send a check to another believer in need, not to a company. I like the feeling that I am helping another believer directly. It isn't classified as insurance but in reality, it functions just like it. There is an amount I pay, specified benefits, and specified conditions that say when I receive those benefits. I only mention this type of plan because some of you may not know about it and I want you to check under every rock before making your health insurance decision.

Final Thoughts On Money

There is a laundry list of poor teachers out there and a long list of people willing to teach you the magical steps for a (wink) small gift, "sewing your seed in their good soil ministry," and telling you how to get more money under the banner of the Kingdom. Each one promises that if you will follow their teaching then debt cancellation and prosperity are yours. The truth is that none of these teachers spend much time correcting the lens that got most people in their dire financial straits. Most of those teachers are preying on people desperate to get out of financial trouble and think that great wealth will fix their problems.

Here is the key concept to understand: anyone who is telling you how to get out of debt without telling you that you are going to have to drastically change the way you spend money in the future is selling you a false god. Oh, they might not know it, but that is what they are doing. They will be selling you some 'kingdom principle' and that if you follow what they say the 'Bible' is saying then God will magically cancel debts and bring windfalls of money.

In actuality, the Bible tells you to avoid debt, work hard, give, save, spend less than you make, and invest (Proverbs 22:7, Proverbs 21:5, Colossians 3:23, Malachi 3:10, Proverbs 21:20, Proverbs 6:6-8, Ecclesiastes 11:2). Beware any spiritual teacher that ask you to give to his ministry as a means of fixing your finances.

If you are currently in financial stress and you don't manage money well, it doesn't mean you are dumb and uneducated. I knew a doctor who kept withdrawing money from his retirement account to pay for a bad land deal he got into. A college education doesn't translate into good money management. "Smart" people make bad money decisions all the time. Handling money well is learned and if you didn't have a father in your life, then money management is just another area that needs repair. You don't have to be a genius to spend less than you make; you just need the lens to drive you toward discipline. Seek help and trust that God will provide. It is okay to recognize money management isn't something you do well. I told one of my sons that the top two things on his list for a wife should be that she loves Jesus and is good at math. It wasn't a joke or jab at him at all. Junior high math isn't his strong suit and when he has kids and they need help with math, life will go well if his wife handles it. The point is that it is impossible to be great at everything so when you find an area in which you struggle, continue to learn and surround yourself with people who can help.

To summarize, get wants versus needs drilled into your head, look to the future, be a giver, and prepare a way for those you love when you are gone.

CHAPTER 4

CHASING GHOSTS

On a drive from Houston to Wichita, Kansas my Aunt Jo said she was going to convince me of two things: that I was white and that I was Roman Catholic. Now there is nothing wrong with being white or Roman Catholic, but her comment made me laugh as she said the words, since both my parents are purely of Mexican descent and I have never had a personal connection with the Roman Catholic church.

Now, many of you have ghosts that haunt you. Your father did this, your grandfather did that. Maybe all the men in your family have had the same troubles over and over throughout the years. There can be things you have to live down or things you have to live up to. Either way, chasing a ghost or running from them is the same problem. It is impossible to destroy something that isn't really alive. You can't kill a ghost. Even if you exorcise it, the memory of it remains. So whats a brother to do? Well for me, that ghost was my father's legacy.

It was my aunt's 45th High School reunion and since her husband had recently passed away in a car accident, she asked me to drive her to Kansas. This was one of my father's four sisters, so I jumped at the chance to serve her and to find out more about where I came from.

My grandfather and grandmother came from Irapuato, Mexico and settled down in Wichita, Kansas back in the 1930's. He worked for the Santa Fe railroad and my Aunt Jo said he preferred Kansas to Texas because of the racial issues in the south. Since my family was not black, they were considered white and got to live 'on the other side of the tracks' in Kansas. My father and his four sisters were all born in a boxcar. Reading the *Boxcar Children* books to my kids always has a familiar feel to me every time I pick up a book because these fictional characters are a shadow of my actual family. My father's family lived in a boxcar until my father was 16 so it is safe to say that he grew up in humble beginnings. We don't have any pictures of that boxcar, but my aunts have painted a pretty good picture of it for me over the years—no running water, no heat, no electricity, but never lacking in anything. My grandmother made their clothes and they never wasted anything.

My Aunt Licho says that my dad (the oldest of the children) was the first to do everything. He was the first to get a job, the first to speak English, the first to go to school, the first to graduate high school, the first to go to college . . . and on and on. I am not sure how much you consider immigrants and how they progress in society but there is always something I noticed growing up: immigrants from some countries come in and hit the ground running, put in extreme hard work, and be a springboard for that first generation to become doctors, lawyers, professionals, and somehow never lose their cultural identity. But when I think about Mexicans as a people, it seems we are content just not being in Mexico. Making more money and living better is balanced by sending money back home yet never striving for more. This is a blanket statement but I always wondered how my people could be here for so long and (racism aside) it take so long get real traction. Why isn't there a larger Hispanic middle class? Why were there so few Hispanics alongside me in my college career? Why are there so few Mexican American degreed professionals my age or older? Why haven't we taken any hold in national politics?

The reason I bring that up is because, during a time when it wasn't easy to be Mexican American and we were not getting real traction beyond citizenship, my father excelled. During my weekend in Wichita, all I heard was how great my father was. Even though this was a younger class, many could recall how different he was. My father, a first generation Mexican American growing up in a boxcar became a leader among his peers. He graduated high school, graduated college, and was commissioned as an officer in the United States Air Force.

During the Vietnam War he was in the Strategic Air Command, in essence helping determine where planes would fly. After the war he worked with NASA on several of their space projects. I was born on McConnell Air Force Base in Wichita, Kansas. Eventually we moved to Omaha, Nebraska and Captain Antonio I. Chavez Jr. had already embodied the success that it usually takes generations to achieve. Sure there were setbacks. My mom told me of how getting the right security clearances were hindered by his parent's nationality despite being legal green card holders. And to this day, I wonder if living next to the Jackson's, a black officer's family, was coincidence or if our living next to them was a bit more intentional. I mean, it was 1975 and there were certainly not a lot of minority officers at that time. The point is, he truly checked the boxes of success: college, master's degree, and was working on a second master's degree when he died. For many, this is not a strange life, but for a first generation Mexican American born in the 1930's, his story is one to marvel at. He was literally born and raised in a boxcar, and despite the lack of lineage, he drove himself to success at a time when the deck was stacked against him.

Now with this broad biographical sketch and with how much I look like my father, you might see how, without anyone saying a word, I had some shoes to fill. I always felt it even if nobody said it. When he died in a car accident in the summer of 1976, my world changed. My father, who in one generation introduced the Chavez family as a legitimate player in chasing the American dream, married my mother who was the opposite.

My mom was originally a Jimenez and they have been here (Texas) forever. My maternal grandparents told me of relatives running with Poncho Villa and how we had land stolen by the Texas Rangers back when stealing land was basically part of their job description. But despite the many years of living in America, there was not much socio-economic or educational progress. Being in Texas meant dealing with some racism, but being Mexican American meant we were only treated better than if we were black. One of my uncles told me a story about my grandmother not being served at a grocery store, but at the same time my oldest brother tells me of her serving black people at the back of their restaurant. Historically Mexicans Americans have been good but not good enough, it seems. My maternal grandfather captained an oil tanker during WWII and when I asked him how a Mexican got to that position, he said because he overloaded the ships and made them money. "When you make them money, people don't care what color you are." I just laughed, but even with that slight success it didn't really translate into any real forward motion for the family, at least not educationally or financially. When he passed away, as with every generation before him, he left no real inheritance or springboard to succeed. My mother's side of the family is filled with emotional, physical, and sexual abuse. My mother was married before marrying my dad because she said she needed "to just get out of the house."

So when my father, who is accomplished and driven, marries my mother, who is uneducated and drifting along, it is easy to see how removing him from the equation set my family's direction back generations. On my mother's side, even though they had been in Texas for generations and generations, I was the first to actually graduate from college. On my father's side, who just got here, I wasn't even the fourth to get a college degree. Oh, don't hear me saying my mom was a burden or education is king. In other chapters you'll find out that what she brought to the table was extremely powerful and that education is just a tool. But looking back,

I wonder how different my life would have been if he had lived to transfer all that drive, determination, knowledge, direction, and wisdom to me and my siblings.

It is easy to see how someone who looks just like his deceased, legendary father might spend his life chasing ghosts. I never wanted to be him and I never felt the need to question God. This was just my life and I just knew that I would go beyond him because I just felt that I would. I never felt comfortable being treated as special. I don't mean people literally treated me better than my siblings but when you walk into a room full of relatives and you look just like your dead father, people just bring it up. That inherently separates you from them and connects you to his legacy, whether good or bad. I never sat down and mentally processed it, it is just something that is automatically internalized and absorbed into one's makeup.

So many of you can relate to this story in some form or another. Some of you are chasing ghosts in order to catch them, others are chasing ghosts in order to kill them, and others just wish you knew where you came from. We say things like: "I'm not gonna be like him", "I'm gonna be just like him", "I'm gonna go further than him", "I'm gonna finish what he started", and on and on.

All of us have been shaped by these ghosts because you just can't escape them, people won't let you, you won't let you.

Well, I am not here to tell you how to do any of those things. This is a practical guide to being a man and being a man means leaving those ghosts behind. You are you and you are not them. There is no reason to chase, kill, run from, or destroy ghosts in your life. These people are part of your story and you were strategically placed in the family you were born into. They key for each of you will be to **embrace your story**, but not in a way that boasts of how you overcame or how you furthered a legacy. The key is to grow more and more into who you already are. You are not them and you are not the sum or their decisions. You are not the past; you are the present. Some of you came into the world by unrighteousness. That means some of you were not born to a husband and wife who desired to share their love with a child to further the Kingdom of God. Some of you were unintended children, born out of adultery, one-night-stands, rape, incest, or just plain "accidents". But you can't dwell on those origin stories. They need to be reframed in your understanding so you can move forward.

You must realize that you might have come through the "wrong path" but your existence is absolutely 100% ordained by God. He is the one who breathed life into your lungs, just as He did to Adam. **Your existence is every bit as ordained as the first man He created**. You entered the world just at the right time, to your exact family (Act 17:26). God is the one who wanted you and He is the one who is writing your story. Life is not created because a man forgets to wear a condom, but because the almighty God ordains life to come into being. Just because He gave you to crappy version of a father does not mean God made a mistake. It means His plans are just beyond your level of understanding. Thus . . . don't chase ghosts.

Instead, fight to discover what He created you to do and you will find that your story will eventually make sense. As I write this, I am 50 years old and it hasn't been until recently that I have understood the absolute goodness of God in the early death of my father. I was never one who questioned Him so I never had the struggles that come from that. I never had anger as some of you have had anger that ended up creating decisions that you wish you could undo. Don't worry, God knew those would come and His story in you will reveal how even those decisions will serve Him and you. Some questions will have answers, and some may never get answered. Trust in God.

I don't ever remember crying about my father's death. Not as a kid, not as a teenager, and not as an adult, but at age 39, I had a weekend where I just could not stop crying. For some reason it hit me that I had outlived him. He was 35 when he died. It hit me that I had now lived longer than him and I had surpassed him in knowledge. I'm talking life knowledge. A 30-year-old with a PhD just can't know what at 70-year-old high school dropout knows because life experience only comes by living. But that weekend I couldn't stop wondering if we would be friends if he had lived. Would the 39-year-old version of me and the 35-year-old version of him get along? Would we agree on sports, politics, raising kids, and so on? Would he like me? I just kept weeping out of control and mourning that I will never know him on this side of heaven. And even if I met him, he couldn't help me because I was older than him. So many times I wish I could call him and ask him what I should do as a father but I can't. Those men who lost their 85-year-old fathers can weep because they no longer have him to ask questions, but men like you and me never had anyone to call in the first place. It is a lonely feeling.

This is what it means to be fatherless . . . to never have and never will. This is the continual sting that you feel. This is why you chase ghosts because you want to know. You want to know who you are. Why do you do what you do? Why did they do what they did? Why didn't they tell you this or that? What should you do about this? How could he leave his biological child? And on and on with unanswered questions. But here is the practical answer: stop asking questions.

It ain't easy but fight to stop asking. God is a Father to the fatherless. You thought you are a never-have and never-will but that isn't totally accurate. You have a Father and you always will. The Old Testament screams of His love for those that have nobody. He will always defend you and *He will* hold accountable those that do you wrong (Deuteronomy 10:18). Let Him handle those who have wronged you because you had no father to protect you. His judgment is righteous and give that over to Him.

But you, oh brother of mine, stop chasing ghosts. My oldest brother Tony, who is actually my half-brother from my mother's previous marriage, still calls my father the greatest man he has ever known. Whatever my father did for him or however well he loved my brother in the five years he fathered him impacted him for life. But I don't know that man. I don't recall that love. In my father's will, he specifically listed my brother Tony as one of his children even though Tony's father was still alive. My dad loved him as a son. Maybe that is why my brother admired him so much. But I don't remember that man and I will never know that man my brother sees as great. All he could have taught me about personal discipline, outsmarting racism, how to be a man, or anything about manhood was robbed from me. I was left without an earthly father and for years I chased a ghost. Even when I wasn't chasing him, he haunted me in the mirror and at every family function where I heard "You look just like your father." Antonio Chavez Jr.'s legacy loomed over me whether I wanted it to or not. That is where many of you find yourself—trapped living up to someone, trapped trying to escape someone's actions, trapped trying to know someone who isn't there, or just trying to reconcile where you came from.

But your freedom will be in chasing your Heavenly Father's legacy. His legacy will shape you in ways your earthly father's legacy can't. Yes, there are practical things you missed out on and it would be good for you to have those lessons but don't worry; God knows, and He is working on your behalf. It may sound hokey but the ghost you need is the Holy Ghost. He will speak to you on behalf of the Father and will shape you where you need to be shaped. The answers are found in discovering who you already are (Chapter 8), rebuilding your life (Chapter 11) and leaving a path for others to follow (Chapter 12).

You have the potential to be the most pivotal man in your family's lineage. Over and over the words "listen to me son, listen to me son," fill the book of Proverbs. As a fatherless father of five children and as one who has been separated from his earthly father just like many of you, I have learned from my mistakes that God can be trusted and His promises are sure. Don't chase the ghosts in your life and as you read this book, glean wisdom from a fatherless father who desires you to be a man who knows how to navigate this earthly world.

CHAPTER 5

SCHOOL DAZE

There is no amount of education that will ever make you wise. In fact, education has the most value when wielded by a person with a heart to bless humanity above self.

I grew up in a time when the prevailing school of thought taught that success meant going to college. With a college education, you will get a good job, make money, and be happy. And if you have a degree from a "good school," getting a good job is pretty much guaranteed so work hard in high school and make sure you get into a good school. In many ways that school of thought is true, but at the same time it can be totally inaccurate. Don't get me wrong, all things being equal it is better to have a college degree than not, but the degree itself does not ensure you of anything in today's world. Economics 101 will inform you that the more there is of something the less valuable it becomes. Dirt is everywhere, so trying to sell dirt just won't get you as much money as selling gold. That is because there is less gold, and since people want gold, it is more valuable. Today, everyone has a degree . . . thus they have less value.

There are three basic types of colleges: public, private for-profit, and private non-profit. Public universities are schools like University of Texas or University of Florida. Schools used to get most of their money from the government, but 2017 was the first year that public schools received more money from tuition than from government funding. And the State is spending less on higher education in 2017 than it did in 2008.[12] A little bonus information is that is one of the reasons for rising tuition is that the state pays less so you have to pay more. Private for-profit schools are schools like DeVry or University of Phoenix. These schools get their money from shareholders and tuition. There is nothing wrong with a school trying to make a profit, but a good recruiter could easily lure a naïve student into a school that makes big promises that it might not deliver, thus Caveat Emptor (Let the buyer beware). And finally, there are private non-profit colleges. These are schools like Harvard or your neighborhood religious school like Southern Methodist University. They get their money from donors and your tuition. They can bring a great value for a student with a pristine academic background because merit-based scholarships can drastically reduce costs. Then again, for someone who doesn't have the resources these schools can smother a student into a mountain of school

12. https://www.cbpp.org/state-spending-on-higher-education-well-below-pre-recession-levels

loan debt relatively quickly. Each type of university has their respective positive and negatives, but all can be disastrous choices for the uninformed high school graduate. It can be a game, but is does not need to be a game you play.

The Game Is Changing

Now, if you are going to be a doctor, lawyer, or engineer of some sort then you must play the game. Getting into the best school and making the best grades makes a difference in what educational opportunities are available to you. There is no alternate entrepreneurial path to become a doctor. You can't just hustle and learn on your own and become a brain surgeon. These types of jobs are only achieved by working within the traditional educational system, so there is great merit in focusing on striving for academic greatness in high school in hopes of getting into the best possible university that you can, in order to graduate from that university so you can have the best possible job options upon graduation. But I'd like to start with careers that have alternate paths.

It is a great time in history for the average joe to make a great living with no college degree or specialized trade skill The internet has removed the gate keepers or entry barriers to so many opportunities. There are YouTube stars that make far greater money and have greater audiences than most actors today. They just simply upload their videos for free and the market determines who watches. There is no casting call, no audition, no talent search; they simply uploaded their video. Similarly, if you wanted to be a columnist and give opinions on the world around you, in the past you had to go to journalism school, pay your dues, show talent, and hopefully get to write your thoughts for a newspaper's particular audience. Today all you need to do is start a blog and you can write whatever you want, how often you want on whatever topic you want. The market will determine if they want to keep visiting, and if there is a lot of traffic, advertisers will pay you to advertise on your site. Want to open a store and sell stuff? Simple; there is no need to rent space and fill it with inventory. No, you can just open a Shopify site and sell product you don't own and have it drop shipped to your customer's home.

The internet has crushed so many barriers to entry in so many sectors of business, and there are now employers who could care less about a degree; they just want someone who can do a job well. Stanford University produces many of the top IT graduates in the world but the companies like Apple and Google have removed their bachelors' degree requirements because they are more concerned that you have the right certifications and skills. I know a guy who doesn't have a bachelor's degree in Computer Science but he has been working in the IT sector since high school. After working at a local company, Microsoft hired him. Now he makes a great living and runs a team of security analysts. It wasn't the degree that opened the door for him and so many others, it was the fact that he had the certifications and skillset they desired. The same opportunities are available in graphic or web design; if you have the skills then you can find a job. These are just a couple of examples of how degrees are not necessary to professional vocational success but believe me there are more.

There has also been an increase in the value found in trade skills. "Blue collar" work lost its' value during the rise of importance of college degrees but that tide is turning too. Welding, mechanics, and other trades have begun to pay much better. The opportunities are rising. On a recent business podcast, I heard a guy say he was having trouble finding guys to work in his commercial refrigeration repair business. He said he would pay them while they trained, and they would easily make 70k a year. Getting paid to learn a trade and then have a guaranteed job has never been the norm but with a growing gap between jobs available and people trained to do them, the market shifted. That is why nurses will get sign-on bonuses – the demand is greater than the supply, so companies have to give incentives for nurses to work there. Why fall into the trap of going into steep student loan dept to get a degree that doesn't provide the same benefit as it did in the past? Not to mention that a lot of people don't even work in the field of their education.

So where am I going with this? If you are young, I want you to consider your options. If you are an entrepreneur, do you need to go into debt to get a degree that doesn't even map toward starting your own business? Is there some other place that you can work or learn that can give you the tools to venture out on your own? Outside of a few jobs like doctor and teacher, I know very few who actually work in the field they received their degree. So ask around, does your degree even map to a job you want? I know a young man right now who just graduated with a public relations degree and marketing minor. Do you know what he is doing right now? He is searching high and low for any job that would help him pay rent. His degree didn't guarantee a job in public relations or in business. He ended up taking a job as a paralegal.

Again, can you get that education somewhere else online or can you just get a website and start that business now? My wife and I have a window covering business and because of my wife's sales ability and my willingness to use my gifts behind the scenes, we do well. She has a degree in marketing and I have a degree in finance. I can tell you that those degrees didn't map to starting up this business and didn't help us start, grow, or market our business. This is how we started—she went to the county clerk's office, got a DBA (doing business as), printed some business cards off Vista Print, picked a supplier, and started knocking on doors. There was no degree required; she just worked. I am not saying starting a business for yourself is easy so just forget about college. What I am saying is that if you have been trained by culture or your parents to fight for a high GPA because that will lead you to the college of your choice and therefore employers will be lining up at your door, that simply isn't true.

You have to think about value.

For instance, going to Harvard above a state university is a no brainer because the value of having a degree from Harvard opens doors and most likely introduces you to people in influential circles, not to mention the possibilities of merit-based scholarships that can significantly reduce tuition. But does going to a state university above the local community college give you a better value? It might on your first job, but you will find that as you progress in your vocational life companies care about who can do the best job not what school you went to. Being a good employee has nothing to do with which school you went to; it has everything to do with what you bring to the table as a person. Do you work hard? Do you have a good attitude? Do you work well with others? Do people like working with you? Do you give your best? Are you a complainer? Those questions are not answered by looking at the school's name on your diploma. Those are answered while on the job. There is a whole industry where headhunters actually call on people to fill a role in a company. They are looking to poach people who produce from other companies.

You have to realize that employers have a much different outlook than during your parents and grandparent's generation. Companies today are not necessarily looking for long term employees. The days of working for one company for your entire career is long gone. They are looking maximize their dollars and if they can find someone to do your job cheaper, then you better believe they will let you go. Take that college graduate with a Computer Science degree. Technology is developing rapidly, so if there is a new coding language or certification needed and you don't have that skill, there is another person they can hire that will fill your shoes nicely, and if they are a recent college grad, they will do it for less. Here is the lesson: you can't just get a job and punch the clock, but you must remain valuable to a company. Hard work and over-delivering never go out of style.

You have to really think and seek wise counsel even when college is the best choice. Let's say you wanted to be an engineer and you lived in Kentucky. Does going to the University of Kentucky give you more value than going to the Colorado School of Mines? You might have to pay out of state tuition but people that graduate from Colorado School of Mines get better jobs because of how companies that hire engineers view those graduates. Then again, certain fields can be booming and then go bust just as quickly. Petroleum engineering was not always a hot field but with fracking and increased exploration, that degree led to great jobs and great salaries. However, when oil prices drop and exploration slows down many of those people could find themselves laid off work and looking for jobs outside of their degree. Of course, that can happen in many fields, but I just wanted to highlight that the US economy might be doing well but that doesn't mean all sectors are doing well. Having no student debt sure does remove the stress of general job insecurity.

Does going to a private school make sense when you know you can't even come close to paying full tuition? Personally, I think it is wrong for a private "Christian" university to let a student amass student loan debt while getting a degree in secondary education. How is a teacher ever going to pay that off? Once again, there is nothing wrong with a private school . . . if you or your parents can afford it. And there are cases where privates school can be less expensive than a public school because each situation is different. But if you want to be different from those around you then remember that none of these universities are forcing kids to take student loans.

Men, life is not a straight path but always looking for the best value will always produce a better harvest. What I want you to do is stop and evaluate your education options before blindly following the cultural path regarding education. Taking out massive student loans to fund a degree that is just not as valuable as it was decades ago is just not smart. Going to a less expensive college over the big one in your state just might be a better decision. As I said, degreed people are everywhere, and those degrees rarely ever map to what you will actually do in the marketplace. Degrees have become more of a certification of completion than job training.

So What Do You Do?

I know, I get it, everyone wants to graduate high school and after a fun summer head off to Universities of Texas, Georgia, Alabama, Tennessee, Michigan, Florida and such. Which one of you wants to hear of a friend heading to one of those schools and turn around and tell them you are staying home and heading to the local community college for two years in order to save money? Who wants to tell those guys that you are making a wise financial decision and working extended hours during the summer so they can pay cash for all their school related expenses? In today's world, who wants to live with the stigma of living at home after high school? Who dreams of being the Tortoise in the *Tortoise and the Hare* story?

Everyone wants to "maximize the college experience" and say they are an alumnus of some "great" school. Who wouldn't want to be a part of Big 10 football games or ACC basketball games? But hear me brother, burying yourself under a mountain of debt for an experience when you can get the same education for less money at another school is folly. The reason is simple: people are the experience above places.

It will always be people that open doors, make connections, and change lives, not locations. Again, learn from my mistakes. I went to school, joined a fraternity, and drunk deeply of all that the college experience had to offer. I visited friends at other schools, did road trips to football

Your eyes won't see enough and your stomach will never eat enough.

games, did spring break in Mexico, and on and on. And all I can tell you now is what you can read in Ecclesiastes—it is all vanity. Those experiences are just vanity because they are physical.

The spiritual always trumps the physical. Being on the summit of the mountain is not complete until it is shared with someone. More than anything, my greatest hope for you when it comes to education is that you would try to follow God. I have known many high school students who have visited colleges as they weighed their options, but I don't know of any that went on the weekend and visited local churches or university ministries. Getting an education at the expense of one's spiritual wellbeing is a trade that will never pay dividends. What I am not saying is that you are wrong if God doesn't come down, give you a vision, or speak to you audibly about your college decision. No, but I am saying is that we should come in prayer, our desires laid aside, and ask God, "Where would you have me go?"

He has not obligated Himself to answer but if you don't begin there, your fleshly desires will cloud your decision. Ignoring wisdom's call to avoid debt, you will ignore simple math that says that community college is cheaper. The fact is that your choice of college alone could save you tens of thousands of dollars. The typical two-year college costs $3,440 annually, while the typical public four-year college costs $9,410 annually and a private four-year college costs

$32,410 annually.[13] That is roughly $12,000 and $58,000 respectively in tuition savings over just two years. Why pay that additional money for core classes like history, English, and political science? Of course you should get the education you feel driven to get and that will help you work in the field you desire, but don't forgo wisdom's call, make poor financial decisions, and then ask God to bless you on the way to that dream university.

Or say you are a father and your son is making his decision on which college to attend. When he pushes back on your direction, you should be able to tell him, "Son, I know what I am saying is opposite of what you are saying but I want you to know something: I am not telling you what I think you should do. I have been in prayer and fasting, laid down my thoughts as best I can, and asked God which path you should follow. So, through prayer and fasting, this is what I *believe* is best for you." Even if he disagrees, you have modeled what it looks like to weigh decisions where there is no right or wrong decision. Both student and involved parents must look to God first so they are not led astray by their fleshly desires masked under the guise of "getting the best education possible."

Getting an education is not college attendance alone; it is also learning how to make choices. Choosing a technical school, university, masterclass, internship or whatever is not a burden but a joy. This is an exciting time because out of it, you will meet new people whom you will be changed by and whom you will change. Relationships will form and ministry

---

13. https://bigfuture.collegeboard.org/pay-for-college/college-costs/college-costs-faqs

will happen. People matter, not location. You will be changed by people you meet, not classes you attend. Be excited to meet new people whether at the community school around the corner or the Ivy League school across the country.

So hear this: **when considering educational options, don't just follow the crowd in how they pick schools.** Whenever possible, consult some wise men who have been down that road. Ask them if there are other paths to do what you want to do. Some of you don't have anyone to ask. It is the information age: find a podcast, a YouTube Channel, or search whatever media platform you can, but look for information beyond yourself. You must get new information so you can actually make an informed decision. You need information to count the cost.

Can you even afford to go to college full time? Is there a school that provides a better value? Is there a trade you would really love to learn that can make a living at instead of going to a university? Ask yourself, "Is my first-choice college really the best decision for me?" Do you need to have a conversation with parents regarding their expectations? That is a big one, by the way. Some of you need to love your parents by letting them know what direction or occupation you really want to pursue.

This is the life God gave you and trying to live to fill their expectations does not serve you or God. There is a difference between dishonoring your parents with your decision and letting them know God has given you another direction. In the same way, some of you parents need to release your children to follow God in a direction you didn't plan. You can't live vicariously through them. Just because you worked hard to give them opportunities you didn't have does not mean they have to take the opportunities you want for them. The difference between controlling your children and influencing them is how much you hear from God. Controlling is when you use the purse strings to make a child do what *you* want. Influencing them is when you let them know those financial resources are available as you believe they are following God. Spending time with God will give your spirit the ability to give them money to do something different than what you want them to or to withhold from them because you truly believe God desires a different direction.

See, there is not a one-size-fits-all scenario because there are so many variables. What type of degree? What resources are available? How certain are you of your ultimate vocational goal? Some of you are stuck because your parents make too much money for you to get grants but not enough to help you pay for school. That is a bad spot to be in when planning to go to university. You have filled out the financial aid forms (FAFSA) and found out you didn't qualify for Pell Grant money (money you don't have to pay back) but are given the option of borrowing the money. It can be a sickening feeling to see the summit but know you can't reach it. Those loans seem like the answer to your prayers; especially if your parents say they will help you to pay them back, but I'm here to tell you that the Tortoise beats the Hare every time. Go to the University of Michigan or UCLA if God leads you there, but find a way to go without borrowing money. The 30-year-old you will thank you. Don't chase experiences. There is no experience at one school that you can't have at another school.

Let me stop and say something to the men who think that time has passed them by: you are not as old as you think. If you never went to college and want to go, then do it. With a wife and kids, you are not going to live in the dorms, but online universities are everywhere. The time has not passed you by, brother. In fact, because you are past making "young man mistakes," you might surprise yourself with what you can do. It might take a few years, but it can be done. I couldn't be prouder of my brother Jeff. He took classes here and there for twenty years, and he got his bachelor's degree at 40. Some people might not find that impressive but that is some real perseverance. He even applied and was accepted into a master's program. He chose not to go but today he is 52-years-old and doing a job he absolutely loves. I just want to encourage you to use the opportunity that wasn't available 20 years ago. In today's world there are schools that cater to working adults; dare to get that degree.

As I close this chapter I want you to hear me say that a college education is not a waste at all but is truly a blessing, and the vast majority of those who read this should pursue a college degree or a vocational school. But some should rethink your top school choice or timeline to complete the degree and none of you should go into debt. The small percentage that don't pursue higher education should make that decision because they have put in the work of researching and planning how they want to make their living. You'll never know what would have happened IF you chose differently so go to that school you have always wanted to attend. Just don't forget to ask God and don't borrow from the future you to pay for it.

A college degree still opens doors in the world we live in but a degree from that local community college won't hinder you. Work is the true currency, not the degree. We will cover it more later, but I can't stress enough that hard work will open more doors than a degree from your dream school ever will. That education you receive at university will likely not prepare you at all for whatever job you get. A plumber's apprentice will learn how to be a plumber but ask around and see how many people use what they learned in college in their daily life. It is an educational system we have in America and that system is broken. There is no new information in statistics since I took that class in 1988, yet the universities charge three or four times more for that same information. Could that information be video recorded and reused? Of course, but that doesn't perpetuate the system. I've placed some book titles at the end of this book to help you see how you can pay for college without debt. None of them are without flaws but all of them call you to the same thing—getting a degree with incurring debt.

Get that education but don't be blind to what it buys. Take your time, be a man, and seek wisdom. My practical advice that I gave to a high school senior last month is to find three men over 50 and tell them your plan. Take a pen and paper with you and write down their thoughts. You don't have to follow their advice, but I can guarantee you will learn something you didn't know that will help you make an educated decision. The young man has a fully engaged mother and father and when she heard the advice, she commented on how smart it was. She didn't fear him seeking wisdom and neither should you.

CHAPTER 6

DEAR MAMA

Gloria Jimenez Chavez passed away on Friday, November 27th. She was born October 1, 1943 in San Antonio to N.F. and Felicitas Jimenez. She worked as a nurse for 22 years, always putting others ahead of herself. During her life she experienced the best and worst that one could experience. But the one thing that towers above all her experiences was the salvation found in Jesus Christ. Gloria lived a Holy Spirit filled life that pointed others to the Gospel of Jesus Christ. She opened her home to anyone in need because she knew Jesus loved "the least of these (Matt 25: 45)." She will be missed by all that knew her.

I had the job of writing my mother's obituary. The above is a portion of it. I give a small glimpse of who she was to those around her. However, the memory below shaped how I thought about her.

Chances are that your mom sacrificed a lot for you. Chances are that woman is your heart. Even if your mom was not the best woman, there is still something for you in this chapter.

We lived out in the country when my father died. There wasn't another house for a mile or so. In the evening it could be eerily quiet, other than the sound of crickets. In that quiet when I was still 6 years old, I heard an uncontrolled wailing behind my mom's bedroom door. And when I mean wailing, I am talking about total loss of emotional control. You remember when you were a kid and couldn't even catch your breath and there was no amount of comfort that would help you stop crying? This was right after my father died and she was feeling the full weight of the loss of her husband. Imagine how hard that would be and imagine if someone couldn't emotionally bear it; that is the sound I heard. And here I was, 6 years old and all I remember was going in, running to her, putting my arms around her, and telling her it was going to be okay and I was going to take care of her. I don't remember her reacting to my words; she was lost in grief and kept crying out in pain. Literally, I can hear everything as I write this. Despite having two older brothers, I felt the sole burden to take care of her fall on me. Now obviously it was ridiculous to think I could fix things but, in that moment, I felt it was up to me.

Now, everybody has a story. My story is not unique, and it certainly isn't the worst anyone ever experienced. I just wanted to give context for where the story goes. My mom wasn't perfect, and we grew up during a time where physical discipline was much more common and acceptable. Throw in the fact that she was a victim of sexual abuse from a family member and that she gave birth to a child that lived just one day, it is totally understandable that she had a lot of pain to work through. But through it all, in the back of my mind, I felt it my job to take care of her.

So fast forward and I finally got to bring those feelings to reality. If you keep up with sports, you have seen the stories of professional athletes buying their moms their own homes. It was a promise they finally got to keep. Well, the first thing I got to do was buy her a car. You should have seen her face as I surprised her. She had no clue it was coming. It wasn't a Mercedes or anything, but it was my first step in being the son I wanted to be. Years later I finally got the opportunity to buy her a house. But before you think I mention this as some badge of honor or in hopes you think how great of a son I was, let me fill you in on the house.

I was on staff at a church making $42K a year and I felt God tell me to buy my mom a house. She was living in a shack of a house just outside my hometown. When I say it was a shack, I am not exaggerating; it could not have been worth more than $10K, including the two acres it was on. Even though she was living in that little place, I wrestled for about six months with God. "God, if I get her a house, how will I get a house when I get married? I want to be able to buy my wife a house when I get married, and I don't make the kind of money to be able to buy another house." Seriously, I argued with God over and over. Thinking of ways I could obey God and still get what I wanted, I even started trying to mentally consider single women at the church who already had a house. Thankfully even in that immature thought process, eventually I'd rule them out for one reason or another. Even still, I didn't move forward with finding my mom a house.

Finally after six months, I gave in and as I did, one of my mom's sister and husband were selling their house. It was great timing and a perfect size. It was a three bedroom with about 1,300 square feet. And here is the really fun part: I didn't know but when I was telling God no and trying every way to figure things out in my head my mom was praying "God, can I have one more house before I die?" My actions were just God's way of providing for my mom before she passed a few years later. And of course, the next year when I got married, I didn't have to worry about buying my wife a house because she already had one. I guess God really knows what He is doing.

What I really can't stress enough is that I know some of you really had great mothers, aunts, aunties, big mommas that you want to pay back. You have high hopes of taking care of them. You really love them and want the best for them. I was like you. I also didn't really appreciate her as I should have when I was growing up. I remember on either my thirteen or fourteenth birthday that I waited all day to get my gift. I knew she had a BB gun under her bed, and I was mad all day because she was sleeping. Yep, she was sleeping all day on my birthday as if it was any other day. She finally woke up and I got my gift, and for some reason we didn't have a cake, but I remember having a big sandwich with a candle to celebrate. I can't remember why there was no cake but like I said, I clearly remember being mad all day because my special day didn't seem so special to her. Now, I look back and think of her working 7 pm to 7 am or 11 pm to 7 am routinely as an LVN (Licensed Vocational Nurse). There I was, a little punk mad because my mom was sleeping and the reason she was sleeping was because she worked all night so I could even have a gift. Oh, what a wonderful mother. It is so sad that she is gone and my kids never got to know her.

So as an adult with the benefit of looking in the rearview mirror, I really wanted to bless her for all she had done and given up for us. I didn't have the resources of some professional athlete but for me and my mom, that car and small house might as well have been a Mercedes Benz and an eight room mansion. Thus, I know the feeling some of you have but you know what, no matter how much I loved her, she could never replace my dad.

Men, I wanted to bring up my mom because, as you read my story I want you to reflect on yours. It is a bit of a gamble because for some of you, it might be a source of pain, but I am hoping that for most of you, the thought of your mother or mother figure stirs up positive emotions. Things you have done for her and things you hope to do for her. It can be complicated because there is never one right way regarding relationships. Each relationship has its own particular twists and turns but historically the relationship between a son and his mom is uniquely special.

My mom was not a great theologian, but her life taught me more about the Kingdom than you can imagine. However, my love for her was never based upon what she taught me. My love for her was solely because she was my mother. That biological connection forged by nine months in the womb can't be underestimated, but she was the one who was there when I skinned my knees and who worked nights doing all she could to make sure we had what we needed. There was no father to take me to soccer practice. Most of you can relate. As we continue moving forward and move into relationships, I wanted each of you to understand that I have nothing but the utmost respect for my mother. She was a true treasure, but she was never equipped to teach me to be a man. At some point every man has to be pushed out to learn to fend for himself.

Picture a young man graduating college or some trade school and yet has to find a job. He has a mother and father and his old room at home is open and he shows up looking for a place to stay. Mom will open that door right up, get him something to eat, maybe have him put his laundry in the laundry room so she can wash it for him. Her instinct is to mother him. On the other hand, that dad might welcome him home but his instinct is to ask him when he is getting a job or what his prospects are so he can go start his own life. His instinct is to push that son to find a job, get a place to stay, and learn what it is stand on his own two feet. Of course mom wants him to find a job and of course dad will be there to catch the boy is he stumbles but at their core, moms and dads are different in how they see a son.

So I want to ensure that as you read about women or moms that you know that my mom was a spiritual giant and a silent teacher in countless ways. She didn't teach me to be a man, but that is okay because she did the best she could. One

As much as I loved my mother and learned from her, she was not a father.

year she said that she deserved a Father's Day gift since she was both mother and father to me. I wasn't being rude or anything, but I told her that that wasn't true. I say that to you because I know that many of you love your mom, aunt, auntie, grandma, big mamma, whoever she is or was. These women loved you and gave all they had for you, but they were not a father and could never be a father.

Oh sure, you learned from them and I am absolutely positive they did everything they could to teach you to be a man, but femininity never bestows masculinity. It just isn't how the world works. I have a daughter and no matter what I do, I can't tell her how to be a woman. I'm just not equipped for that job. At best, I can tell her what I think a woman should be and give her a male's understanding of femininity and how to live it out. Similarly, that is all that a woman can give to you—a female's understanding of masculinity.

I was disciplined by my mother but she didn't teach me to be disciplined; there is a difference. In the next chapter we will tackle relationships. Not having a father sets us up for failure and even though we might have had a great mom, she still might have contributed to our personal failures in relationships. Despite this, take a second, be thankful for the mother who raised you, and maybe even call her. As you read the next chapter reflect on all you missed out on because she could not do what a dad does. There is no need for you to communicate to her that she wasn't enough; in fact that would probably be extremely rude.

You need to be able to appreciate what she did for you, honor her, and be thankful to God for her, but you also need to notice that God's design was something else. Letting go of mom and trying to be a man is necessary. That strength, confidence, and conviction found in a man who knows who he is irreplaceable. A man who knows himself is even secure in the fact that he doesn't know everything. The older you grow the more you realize how little you know. The best you can do is know enough to help someone and appreciate all those who taught you along the way. That mother or mother figure is or was a blessing that can't be ignored.

Make sure you thank them for the love and wisdom they passed along.

CHAPTER 7

FEMALES AND FRIENDS

Show me your friends and I'll show you your future. That isn't absolute truth but where there is smoke there is fire. The same can be said for the saying "Hurt people hurt people." We all need to take our relationships a bit more seriously considering how much people around us affects our lives and how much we affect them as well.

We become what we behold. If we had grown up with a wonderful father who loved a wonderful mother, we would all have a different view of women in all of our relationships. To see him speak kindly to her, put her needs above his own, yet at the same time seeing him bask in her respect for him, we would have had a better relationship history in every area of our lives. Instead, for many of us, our view on male-female relationships is a Frankenstein mess, pieced together by so many components. We have been taught by the culture, our mom, our friends, watching our friends, their parents, movies, and on and on. In addition, our choice of friends is rooted in people that like us more than people we want to be around.

One of the things that subconsciously get hardwired into boys who grow up without a strong male in the home is a skewed view of love and relationships. It becomes almost automatic to love mom but not necessarily love girls. With nine months in the womb and the sacrifices we have seen her make for us, the connection makes sense. It also makes sense that mom gets real love, while girls end up as a source only for physical pleasure and not for intimacy and vulnerability. There is an insecurity that won't allow a real intimacy because without that strong father, a boy won't really know who he is, is unsure of himself, or puffs himself up with other things to compensate. But even that absentee father would tell a son not to get a girl pregnant or hand him condoms without any other instruction because *dads always have something to say.* Dads are naturally hard on boys and soft on daughters. Mothers, on the other hand, are hard on daughters but soft on boys. The reason is because dads know firsthand what they are preparing their sons for and moms know firsthand the issues women face, so without that dad, you end up with missing parts of the puzzle. I'm not saying a strong single mom can't do anything to make a man, but she is not built to be both a mother and a father. This is part of the problem.

Young women are not competition in a father/son relationship. But that strong single mother can become either a natural protector for her "baby" or she may swing the pendulum the other way—be his friend and point out to him women of interest. Now, there is nothing at all wrong with a healthy mother/son relationship. In fact, when paired with a strong father, it is part of the equation in developing a boy into a man. The problem arises when that father is removed and all that is left is that strong single mother. That developing man's lens is skewed and his relationships will be affected for years to come.

So many young women have been hurt and wounded by boys with a feminized masculinity. Women become commodities: things to conquer and sources of pleasure, instead of gifts to be treasured. Often if there was a controlling mother, then women become people to dominate by men. Mom in her strength tells him what to do and not do all day long and the result: he ain't letting some girl run his life. Nope, instead he is going to dominate her. Avoiding intimacy is what will manifest because that man will do anything to not be controlled by a woman again. So a guy in this group may look for women he can control as a means to not be controlled.

Even those men who have a mother who is absentee herself leaves her son in a skewed mentality. Without that strong father and with now paired with an uncaring mother, that boy won't know who he is and end up finding a woman to "mother" him. What I mean by that is, that guy will date girls who tell him what to do and take care of him, or he will redirect all that anger on some or many young women. The old saying that wounded people wound people is a true one and unless you spend time getting "right" as a man, your relationships will suffer.

Brothers, you have to be honest with yourself and understand that femininity never bestows masculinity. That is what I am talking about when I say feminized masculinity.

Without strong dads, boys will either try to shape themselves into men or a mother will try to do it for them. Fill in this blank: "Just wait till your ________ gets home." This isn't a statement made by weak women. There is just a different response a boy has to his father or a man in general. We got swats with a paddle in public school when I was a kid. My guess is that beginning in 2nd grade, I got upwards of 100 swats, but not one was from a male. Those male coaches got my best behavior because I wasn't about to catch one from a 6-foot man. Look, single women have raised presidents from George Washington to Barack Obama, but achievement doesn't define what is inside a man any more than sexual conquests. In fact, President Obama's own biography reveals all the questions he had in as a man because his father wasn't really in his life.

It is hard enough for a father grow a man so to ask a woman to do so is an unfair, yet that is plight of many. And it will affect your female relationships. Look back on your life. Have you been a womanizer with no real intimacy? Have you tried to be close but unable to actually give and receive love? Have the women in your past been unhealthy, mothering care takers? Are women to be valued or just there for your pleasure? Do you feel insecure until you have enough sex? Do you have a history of dominating women but don't really know why? Ever find yourself never being "good enough" in relationships? When pushed toward intimacy, does anger come out in order to push her away? Do you look for women more broken than you to feel secure? There are so many questions that reveal the real problem. A father doesn't instill who you are; he identifies it, lets you know what is in you, and shapes you for the challenges that lie ahead for the man you will become.

I am 100% positive that many reading this have a wake of destruction behind you. That doesn't necessarily mean there is a list of abused women in your past, although for some that is true. I am saying there are women who you told wonderful things to in order to get sex, only to ghost them later. I am saying many of you used women like hats, trying them out to see if they fit you. Because your father didn't teach you to truly value a woman, you allowed yourself to scar them emotionally. You preyed on their insecurities and you validated them when left them to pick up the pieces. You told yourself that she was a big girl and she wanted sex just as much as you.

The really hard part is that one day, if you are not already, you will be dealing with the aftermath of what other guys similar to yourself did to your wife before she met you. That spouse or future spouse will have wounds from guys just like you that will need to be healed. Life will come full circle, but when it does, if you know who you are and have learned the value of a woman, you will do all you can to be an understanding M-A-N.

The things I mention are not off-the-wall statements; just google "effects of fatherlessness" or something similar. Now, you can read this and disagree with the inner workings of all this. The point is not to do some psychoanalysis of a general group of men. My hope is to point to the tip of the iceberg and help you deal with the larger part of the iceberg underneath the water. You don't need me to tell you anything. What you need to do is ask yourself simple questions and pay attention to how you answer those questions.

What should I do?

There are so many questions you could ask: "Why do I relate to women the way I do?" "Did my father's absence and my mother's style of mothering warp my internal workings in a way that is unhealthy?" "Do I look to dominate women or be led by them?" "Can I be overly passive in my decision making?" "In past relationships, has my wife's or girlfriend's opinion been my north star or what I won't listen to at all?" "Despite my job, success, physical appearance, and the positive way people view me, am I secretly driven by fear and insecurity?" "Is it possible that my pornography problem emanates from the lack of healthy fatherly influence and unhealthy female influence?"

These are just simple questions that will most likely stir up some questions in your mind. The practical thing I want to focus on is that these questions should just help you really embrace that there is an issue to address. The issue won't be resolved by reading this or any book. You go with you. The issue will be resolved by working to identify how not having a healthy, loving set of parents in the home has affected you. And once you have done that, it will take some time to unlearn one way of living and be transformed into more of who you were intended to be.

Getting rid of one girl and picking up another won't help because another woman won't make you another man.

Picture a fight between two men. Men don't want to kill but they certainly don't want to die, so in a fight the desire to not die might drive a man to kill. In the same way, men will do a lot of things in order to *not have other things happen.* Men will lie to a woman rather than be known and possibly rejected. Men will lie about their conquests, not to brag, but in order to avoid humiliation. Men do a lot of things to avoid something more painful. It is just our nature.

You are a complex person that no *one* person can understand. That is where God comes in. Let Him lead the way and He will transform you into the best version of yourself. That transformation can come with the help of a male mentor, a group of friends, a biblical counselor, etc. There is not one way to do it; just be intentional about shedding off the old self and look forward to continually putting on the new you each day. Some of you may not relate to or agree with what I am saying, but I still want to share it with you.

Why change?

Some of you really don't see a problem and that is okay, so I want explain why because if you understand that, then it won't matter if you see a problem in your life or not. In 2 Timothy 2:20-21, God speaks of people cleansing themselves in order to be used. He isn't talking about salvation or being righteous; He is talking about holiness. A believer will never be more or less righteous because righteousness is 100% bound up on Christ's work. Holiness is different. Holiness is about being set apart for God's use. You need to change or clean yourself up, if you will, so you can be more useful to God's purposes. This isn't about you. Once again, this is about others. You *love your wife as Christ loves the church*

(Ephesians 5:25) if you are more Christ-like. Male-female relationships are something we all need to work on. The world has tainted things and we need to be cleansed.

I remember when I first got that revelation. Growing up, I never saw my grandfather get his own plate of food. My grandmother always fixed his plate of food, and when she passed away, my mom or one of my aunts got his food for him. Engrained in my mind was the idea that I wanted a woman that would serve me. It wasn't something taught to me, it was just culturally infused into my way of thinking. Later, while I was reading the Bible, I saw Jesus laying down His life for His bride, the church, and it dawned on me: I never should have seen my grandmother get her own plate. My grandfather should have been serving her. It wasn't wrong that she did it or that my other female relatives did it, but once I got a new perspective, my thought process when dealing with women began to change. They became people to serve, not serve me.

The lone point I want you to get from that story is that my Mexican American cultural influence absolutely shaped how I viewed women and their place in my life. I am not saying there is anything inherently wrong with a woman taking care of you in that way, but I can guarantee you that you too, have been shaped, informed, and molded by your what you beheld growing up, the culture you are a part of, and your own selfish desires. Some of those things need to be changed, and unless you actively lay those on the table, you will feel the ill effects of them in your life, if you have not already. Divorce is common today and it will be on the menu as long as you live with a selfish lens or have horrible relationship skills imbedded in your brain.

Ever wonder why a male celebrity will leave a "hot" actress for a "less hot" actress? The answer is simple: **men don't need better, men need different**. That is why the weekend hunt for our next prey isn't about finding a wife, but about us getting someone different. That is also why men convince themselves that if they divorce their current wives, things will be better in their next marriage. We believe different *is* better.

So expand your mind, let someone peek behind the curtain, and seek change.

It isn't about doing things; it is about being and seeing in a new way. Ask a friend for his thoughts on how you treat women. Be honest: tell him you are looking to improve as a person. You don't have a friend that you feel comfortable asking that question? Then find one. You have nothing but friends that would laugh and call you soft or weak if you ask for help? Then get some new friends who actually want what is best for you. That is the other group you need to consider anyway.

Friends

You also really need to understand your friendships. Like most relationships, our friendships develop during our life and we all move on from some friends and add new ones along the way. There are different seasons in life that can bring new friends and move us away from other friends. All of this is a part of life that everyone navigates. But here I want to focus on something tangible. What does the relationship with your friends produce or provide in your life?

Your relationship choices will really impact your life more than you think. Too often we let life happen to us instead of being proactive. I'm not saying to go find that special group of people that will help you succeed in life, but your belief system is shaped by people around you. I heavily influence my children by pointing them to God in all things. I want them to become dependent upon Him alone, so I try to model it, point to His sufficiency and His great love for them. At the same time, when my kids are away at school, especially as they get older, those friends start influencing them. Their speech can be affected, the questions they have about life are impacted, and even their thoughts about themselves can change. Like it or not, everyone is shaped by the world and relationships around them.

Practically speaking you must stop and really do an inventory on what you believe and why. How have you been shaped by your friendships and are the results positive? I'm not talking about cutting out the friends that don't add value but about stopping and asking yourself the questions: "Why do I think the way I do? Do I have a positive attitude about life, or do I think that success and happiness are for other people? How have the people around me shaped those thoughts?"

Look, plenty of men have found friends who are more family to them then their own family. From neighborhood gangs to college fraternities, the sense of belonging is comforting when you have nobody else. There is safety and protection in being a part some organized group of your peers. But my call to you today is to consider your friends—where do they lead you and what do they want for you?

The "I'm keeping it 100 and rolling with my crew" mentality is fine if you never aspire to something beyond your small world. Many professional athletes have lost their careers by "keeping it 100" and refusing to let go of some of those old friendships. If all your friends don't have anything going on different from you, what do you think you can learn *from* them?

Once again, the point is not to do an inventory of your friends in order to consider who to cut out. The point is for you to ask yourself who you want to become and how you plan to get there. Continually hanging out with the guy who always complains about how bad he has it will not propel you forward as much as the guy who always looks at the positive.

You don't need to sell out. You need to invest in yourself by surrounding yourself with some friends that propel you forward; people that you can learn from. Maybe you can be the positive voice to that guy who is always negative, but when you are the only one telling you that you can do it while surrounded by others saying it can't be done, then you will eventually be shaped by their voices. Find people and groups that will expand your worldview for the better. You have to learn the difference between a friend that you hang out with and that friend who actually wants the best for you *and can help.* I had plenty of college friends saying, "Come on, Chavez, just one drink" knowing I had a test the next day. They really wanted me to come hang out and have fun, but none of those guys really wanted what is best for me. Of course they were not bad friends and we had plenty of good times but I lived in ignorance, thinking that having "fun friends" and surrounding myself with 'real friendships' was essentially the same.

I was a child living as a man and that is what I hope to help you avoid. Live as a man and understand that the people you surround yourself with make a difference in your life.

Ask questions of people that know things in areas of life that you want to learn. You don't have to become golfing buddies, but you will be amazed by how relationships can develop by just asking people questions.

You will always have different friend groups in life. Some people will always be in your life, not because they add value but just because there is some kinship that keeps you connected even when you don't see each other often. And yes, of course there are people that you probably need to cut out of your life, but please don't hear me say that once you get rid of bad people and add good people, life will go well. That is a totally self- centered approach to life.

Within your friend groups you should be able to pour into some people the things you know while also being poured into by others. See, if you want to be a whole person you always have to consider giving to others out of your knowledge and experiences. Even a dumb high school kid knows more than a smart junior high kid when it comes to life experience. He may not know algebra better, but he has navigated waters that younger kids don't even know exist. You too have something to offer. At the minimum you can tell people what not to do, but you have to be on the look-out for people to help.

People are crucial for success in all areas of life, from career to finding a spouse. The people you meet and become friends with can help or hinder you in countless ways. But the key to being a good friend is not being a taker, meaning that the characteristic you are known for is always taking and not giving. There is always that one guy who always seems ready for someone else to pay for lunch. You know the guy. He has his hand on his wallet, but he is just hoping that someone says, "Don't worry, I got it." Don't be that guy.

They key is to actually look to be friends, not somebody out networking in order to get ahead in life. There are networking groups out there and I'm not saying it is inherently wrong to get to know more people who might be mutually interested in helping each other succeed, but inherent in that system is a self-serving motive. You will find that the more you serve people, the more people want to know about you.

This type of discussion is not revolutionary but sometimes the obvious solutions are hiding in plain sight. The fundamentals are always important and when you forget them, problems arise. Spend less than you make, listen more than you talk, look before you leap, and on and on. Listen brother, this is simple, and you were probably told it by someone along the way if you didn't know it already: be mindful of who you hang out with because it does matter. Don't deceive yourself. Many of our relationship failures happen because we lie to ourselves. We know that girl is a bad choice or that one friend is going to get us in trouble, but we say to ourselves it's not a big deal and we can handle it.

Or maybe you put on a mask and pretended to be someone you are not and ultimately you end up unhappy because you are not living your own life. This is the framework for a lot of divorces; a man thought he could be what he presented but in the end, he was too selfish to actually be who he vowed to be. Once again, that deep insecurity that came from not having a father is like a small water leak. It may take some time to cause problems but eventually it will manifest and cause problems we could have avoided if we just fixed the leak.

Before ending the talk about friends, I don't want to forget to mention the obvious answer to the question, "Where can I find new friends?" Being involved at a local church is a great place to cultivate friendships. There are Bible studies, men's groups, and other opportunities to meet other men and become friends. Some churches even try to match younger men with older mentors. One of the blessings in finding new friends at a local church is there is the shared interest in keeping the Kingdom of God central in your life. Wanting the best for others is a key theme in the Kingdom and that idea needs to be incorporated into every area of your life. You can't make new friends magically appear, but you can ask God to send them. One of my college drinking buddies had his life changed by God, and when we reconnected he was married so our life stages didn't really mesh. But he prayed with me that God would send me some buds and God answered. Another time, I was in a new city with no real relationships and because God is good, He provided what I needed. I went to the VA to get my shoulder checked out, and I ended up talking to the doctor for two hours that day. I walked out with a new friendship that has sustained me for the last several years.

Start asking God to bring new friends. He will do it because He is just that kind.

Family

Before ending this chapter centered on relationships, I want to say something about family. How many kids have been shaped by parents telling them they were not good enough throughout their lives? The family that should have been a part of the solution ended up being one of the major problems. Verbal jabs calling your dumb, stupid, fat, ugly, or whatever negative comment they could think of eventually added to your view of yourself. You are not defined by those negative comments, but in order to move past them and keep them in the rearview mirror, you will need to replace them with positive comments. Great friends are needed in life and they can really fill the void left by negative parents. If you don't have those great friends now, I highly suggest you become that for others. Be a treasure hunter and look for ways to complement those around you.

I'm not saying that you should fawn over your boy's jump shot. I'm just saying if you see that he is hitting more jump shots then just let him know that you noticed. "I see you've up'd your game lately. Those shots are falling all the time now. Show me what you're doing." Something as simple as complimenting a small change and reinforcing it by asking how he did it will go a long way. Be that guy.

CHAPTER 8

DISCOVER WHO YOU REALLY ARE

Your mission if you choose to accept it: leave who *they said* you are behind and reach for who *you could be* instead.

There is a certain unspeakable joy when you are able stand in front of the mirror, look directly into your own eyes, and stand content with what you see. For most of us, it won't be until the man looking back at us is grey and weathered, but regardless we all need to strive to know and love the man in that mirror.

This is the hardest chapter to write in the practical sense because there isn't a list of things I can tell you to do. Becoming and discovering who you are is not done by going down a checklist. Knowing who you are will be a road straightened out over time and through experiences. In the

Bible, Abraham was actually a grown man when he left his father's house. That is when his journey to understanding that he will be a man of faith began to unfold, and it began to unfold through mistakes (Genesis 12). His story is one of faith. To have faith revealed means he had to have the opportunity to utilize faith, and his faith was revealed through his success and failures. You don't exercise faith once and possess forever. Faith is an ongoing action. You can think you believe, but you won't know that you believe until you actually have to live in that belief. Similarly, even if you had a great father, it is time and experience that will reveal to your own heart what God put in you. This is what it means to become who you are. So when you are young, try, experiment, fail, leap without looking, but never do anything contrary to the revealed word of God—going after quick money, being crafty, greedy, or a swindler.

I can recall a story that helped me begin to understand who I really was—when I was in about 7th grade, my church youth group sold candy to raise money. I have no idea what we raised money for, but I do remember selling the candy door to door. We are talking about 1982, so this is well before the internet and the availability of information at your fingertips. We actually used a telephone book or called 411 for information to find out a number to call when you wanted to reach a business. I don't know how I got the information, but I found out where the church ordered the candy. After I sold a box of candy, I called the company and ordered some more candy. I used those proceeds from my door to door selling to buy a box of candy for myself. When I went door to door selling candy for the church youth group,

I said something like, "I'm selling candy to raise money for my youth group." Now with my small-town set of morals I didn't go around using that phrase when I sold that second box of candy. Nope, I just tweaked it to, "I'm selling candy to raise money." See the subtle change? I wasn't lying, I just wasn't honest that I was raising money *for me.*

I know, I know. What kind of young con man takes money from the church to fund his schemes? First off, I gave the church back their money and kept mine . . . no harm, no foul. Alright, I know it was wrong but there is a reason I share that story. What is inside me is not a thief or con man. What is in me is a set of eyes that sees opportunity and notices things that other people don't see. My problem is that without a father to identify that within me and point it in a positive direction, I lived my life and never knew how to harness that gift, mostly because I didn't really know it was a gift to serve others.

To me, I was who I was, and I assumed everyone saw the things I saw. I just didn't get how unique my sight was or that it was put inside me for others. That gift just lived in me and manifested in hundreds of ways growing up. While playing soccer, beyond physical talents I could always see openings in the defense or ways to attack without the ball. In my dealings with people, I could get under people's skin easily because I could spot an emotional weakness. Even as I entered college it came out. My undergrad degree was in finance because I thought I wanted to be a stockbroker, but as I took those classes, the concepts were difficult for me to grasp. However, there was a finance track that did appeal to me. It was the track that had me analyze how best to utilize a piece of land, building, or another commodity. Finding the best value for something fit me. Seeing possibilities or having unique insight came natural to me. It isn't some special spidey-sense or anything like that, it is just how God made me.

See, part of what is in me is the ability to see differently than others, but how to utilize that gift is not a plug and crank equation. That gift can be poured into so many different occupations. I could be a consultant, buy and sell real estate, teach the Bible, be a coach, or a lot of different things. Someone who has a gift of caring for people could be a doctor, pastor, counselor, nurse, or many other occupations, but at their core it is their care for people that will be front and center. Too often we get caught up on an individual occupational calling instead of realizing that it is what is inside (our gifts) us that is more important.

And what is inside us is given for us to serve those around us. Too often most of us just don't know what is inside of us. I could have just as easily been a great criminal mind as I could have been a loss prevention specialist. In fact, I would contend that most thieves have a gift of seeing opportunity and steal due to other factors. I'm not talking about the guys who just randomly sees someone, pulls out a weapon of some sort, and robs them. I'm saying there are many who commit crimes, and it is something innate in them that helps them commit those crimes. Many a drug dealer has a talent for business in them that is poured into the wrong vessel. So many have gifts or talents that are misused because what they do naturally has never been identified and pointed in the right direction.

Of course I am not saying there is only one singular gift inside each person. Every person is complex and has many gifts and abilities inside them, but the more we know about ourselves, the closer we are to having a vision. Who you are will help drive the vision, not the other way around. Most of us have been directed, redirected, shaped, nudged, and shut down by people since childhood. People have told you what you can do, what you can't do, and what you should do for so long that it is difficult to know what is right. And depending upon your personality, you might have decided to be what someone said *you are not* just because they told you that you couldn't do it. Similarly, others have been chasing or trying to kill ghosts for so long that who they are is mostly defined by who they are trying to live up to or live down to. All of this results in men who are made in the image of the world around them more than who God made them to be.

Let's pause for a second and chat about that. God intentionally put you in a family line at a certain point. According to Acts 17:26, He chose who would be your father and when that would take place. That means you are not a mistake. That means you are not a mistake (repeated intentionally). That also means that you are not responsible for what came before you. You are not them. You are responsible for what you do with you. Just because they sinned does not mean you have to make up for it. Their sins will affect your life up to a certain point because we live in a physical world. If your father left your mother in dire straits, then most likely you will be broke growing up, but that does not mean you have to live in poverty for the rest of your life. Or if your father was abusive to your mother and you had to watch it growing up, that means you will have emotional wounds, but that does not mean those wounds are incurable.

You have the parents God chose for you, flaws and all; let it go. Some of you may have had things done to you or have seen things a child should not have seen, but God is big. **He heals the broken hearted. It is what He does**. The chapter on rebuilding and repairing will cover this more, but it needed to be touched on here so we can uncover who you really are.

A degree or job won't tell you who you are and until you know who you are, it will be difficult to even ask the right questions. And without a father helping you know who you are, the more insecure you will be. Insecurity can lead to false boasting, looking for approval, false pride, or low pride. False boasting means you try to make yourself look like you have it together when you are really don't. The insecurity of not knowing who you are will make you follow the world or people, thinking you are becoming who you need to be. In reality, you actually didn't need to change but you needed to become more of who you are.

I remember clear as day a decision in the 10th grade: I had just moved schools so I was the new kid, and there was a girl who was interested in me, and my flesh wanted to jump at the chance. But I was in classes with all the smart white kids and that was the same crowd who were headed in the direction I wanted to go. Like I said before, it wasn't a calculated plan but more of an internal instinct. The girl that liked me was not part of that crowd and as the new kid, I felt I had to make my choice count and forsake my teen desires to find success in the future. It wasn't about being "cool," it was all about trying to get on the same path as the successful kids. And that began what amounted to probably a fifteen to twenty year span of me trying to fit into a system that I thought would bring about success. Looking back, I know why I thought that way. Public schools began offering honors classes during that time and those are the classes I took. In my three years at that school I was the only Mexican in those classes. There was one African American and one Korean, and the rest of the students were white. It wasn't that I shouldn't have taken those classes and it wasn't that those friends didn't turn out to be good friends; they were. It was that I thought I had to bend or conform who I was to become successful. I thought I couldn't be me and succeed. *The reality is that being me is success.* Now that certainly doesn't mean I should have chosen that girl. In fact if I had a father, I probably would have avoided her for other reasons, the main one being that I was still just a boy.

I'd like to highlight that those fifteen to twenty years were not necessary, and my great hope is to help you avoid losing that much time. It wasn't that one decision, but decision after decision after decision that led me down the path that delayed me from really knowing and becoming who I already am. Of course, it would be easy to say I was a sellout but when you don't know who you are, selling yourself short is worse. Selling out is turning your back on a group to gain something.

Selling yourself short is when you conform to what others think you should be because you drastically underestimate your own value.

Many of you are on the same path or have been on the same path for years. You have let the world, friends, and family shape you. In small ways you gave up who you really are so you could fit in, not to be popular but because it just seemed like the path to follow. And now, years later that marred identity has become some much a part of you that you don't know who it is that stares back at you in the mirror each day. But that guy is so familiar that you are really scared to find out who he really is. What if people don't like him? What if he fails? What if they know his fears? What if all the excuses are gone and you still are not successful? What if you change and things fall apart?

Don't let what you are now stop you from being what you could be (become who you are). The path of least resistance will never bring change but if you will allow yourself to dream, you will find that the real you are more powerful than this tainted version will ever be. There is great freedom in knowing who you are and being absolutely comfortable with it. If these words ring true in your spirit and you feel like you have given up who you really are along the way or you just don't know who you are, that is okay.

Your life has themes. Good and bad, examine your life and really pay attention. Where do you remember making a decision that you really wouldn't make today, not because of the negative impact of that decision but because the decision just wasn't you? There are plenty of those decisions and when you consider them you will begin to unveil more of who you are without all the changes. It will take time, and no matter what your background or how great your upbringing, everybody grows and gets to really know themselves as they grow older. The point is that there is not a destination to find out who you are but a journey to be on to appreciate who you were made to be.

Suffering and success can both attribute to not really knowing yourself. Suffering can lead to bitterness and living in resentfulness keeps you from forgiveness and leaves you a victim. To really be who you are, you will need to embrace that God was there in that suffering and it can be for your good if you will let Him lead you to it. If you can just be willing to be willing to trust Him in that, you will be able to move towards forgiveness, which will release all that bitterness and resentment. Oh, the freedom that comes when the victim does not stare back at you in the mirror! That man, the free man, is a conqueror. He has conquered the things done unto him and sees it as a chapter in his story, but not the theme of his life.

Success on the other hand will mask the issues you have in your heart for a while, but they will eventually come out in your life. Day by day, people will complement you on things you have accomplished and what you have overcome, but deep down there is an insecurity that only you know. Part of the problem is that because everyone sees you as successful, you can't really let them know how you really feel because that would destroy the illusion of your success. And without that success, what will you have and who will you be? Will anyone accept you if you are not the guy with success? Your freedom is found in letting go of the façade and trusting that you are enough without success. The truth is that success is part of the illusion. Accomplishments of any sort don't define someone's personhood. The culture loves to label someone as success but just as quickly they also label someone a failure. The truth is that what you do is never who you are. You are not a success or a failure, you are you and you are enough. You are enough because God made you and people's opinions are fickle. Today they love you and tomorrow you are yesterday's news. Find the freedom found in identity not tied to earthly accolades.

Yet still, some of you look in the mirror or compare yourself to others and feel like a failure or that you don't measure up. A major problem is that you are putting yourself in the place of God by determining and defining failure and measuring success. Let me tell you about one of my uncles who was drafted to the Vietnam War. Upon his return, he had some severe issues that were created from his time in war that manifested themselves for the rest of his life – problems with the law, addiction, and all the chaos that comes with it. If you were to judge him by the world's standards, you might say the war took the best of who he was. But I don't see it that way. See, we were all given a measure of faith and despite all the terrors that the Vietnam War imposed on my uncle, he never gave up. He would get knocked down, fail, and yet he would eventually limp back to God in hope. He was prayed over countless times and countless times he would fail, but still he never gave up. I can't speak for my entire family but I believe he was considered the black sheep of the family. Yet when I remember him, all I remember is how he never lost faith.

It was easy for some to come back relatively unphased. For others, it took years of counseling to conquer those events. And for others, they never recovered mentally or physically. I truly believe my uncle exhausted all the faith that was given to him just to make it to the end of his life still holding onto God. Externally he might have looked like a weak Christian, but he was actually the one using all he had to remain faithful. The point is that perspective frames what we see. Some could see my uncle and see wasted life, but that man is an example to me of who a man of faith is – someone who puts all hope in God.

The thing is that you are not the judge, not even of yourself. It is easy for me to not have severe anger issues because my father died when I was young. It isn't something I did, it was just the measure of faith God gave me. That doesn't mean my other brothers and my sister handled things the same way. We are different people with different issues, faults, strengths, and weaknesses. Don't compare yourself to someone or even compare yourself to the image of who you think you should be. No, instead just try to be faithful. The sooner you let go of comparisons and focus on today, the sooner your tomorrow will bring about changes in you that you never dreamed were possible.

It is said that it isn't a cave that brings fear, it is what you bring into the cave through your imagination. Those fears will keep you from confronting that victim or success in the mirror, but that fear you have in your mind is not real. It can feel like you are alone in that cave at times but in time you will learn that God is in the cave as well, so you are never alone. There is peace when that realization drops in your heart.

So what can I deliver practically to help you find that peace? Well, you can't mimic someone's behavior in order to get what they have. You must know how they think in order to understand their behavior. Even still, you need to follow your path not theirs so just glean from them in order to help propel yourself. Mimicking someone's behavior seems to be man's default. "How did he accomplish XWY? Well, I'll just do what they did, and I'll get XWZ too." The world doesn't work like that. As I said, you have to know why they do it in order to be able to glean from how they do it.

Fix your reason for why you want change. For instance, if you are tired of being the victim and want to change, you will have a wrong motivation. You will be trying to run from that victimized person or kill that person to become someone new. Instead, you want to be transformed. By that I mean, that being victimized is a component of who you are today and that is okay. Instead, you want to be motivated to be the best you possible and desire change for that reason. That victimized person can be in your past and **he is part of your story; he just wasn't the defining person in your story.**

The same is true for the successful person and everyone else in between. You want to be the best version of who *you are*, not the ones shaped by the world. Wanting the best version of yourself starts with not fearing what you might lose. The practical might mean counseling or it might just mean that you start making small decisions based on who you want to be rather than who you are today. It all starts with being honest with yourself and looking back in your life to begin to reveal where you started selling yourself short. Maybe you spent 5 years or 25 years walking down a path paved by the world's influence. That is ok because the your story, your book is still being written and the upcoming chapters are the chapters of redemption, victory and passing the torch.

Any great success story has chapters of pain, challenges, failures, highs and lows. You are the hero in that story and the sooner you shake off the old you, the sooner that hero begins to rescue others. Who you are is about others. Free people *free* people.

Final Words

There is great freedom in being who you are and feeling zero need to apologize for it. I'm not saying you are free to be worldly. You have to strive to be godly. Becoming the guy who "keeps it real" at the expense of others isn't you; that is a worldly you. When God created you, already knowing your family history and your life experiences, He still had in mind who you could become. The best version of yourself points to Him. "Look at this one. This one I found abandoned, hurt, bruised, and without hope. But now look at him; he is transformed and today never has to edit who he is or hide who he is, yet he is still kind, loving, and considers others greater than himself." Becoming who you are is about no longer editing yourself or hiding part of yourself because you fear what others think. There is freedom in just being yourself. You are free to be you without a mask.

CHAPTER 9

GOTTA WORK IF YOU WANNA EAT

WORK—the sacrifice of the present for the fruit of the future.

We all must sacrifice the present because we all have to work. Yet even in work, fatherless men still need another lens, a lens an intentional father instills. Think about this: how many scholarship athletes have quit after their first year? Prime opportunity! Free education, room and board, playing the game, they love but they didn't like the coach, the lack of playing time, the way they were treated, or whatever . . . and they quit the team. Here they are on the cusp of getting a way out of their circumstances and being a part of a team, yet regardless of all that they return home of their own volition. Why don't they just stay? Simple, the lens with which they view life allows them to quit.

I don't know the statistics, but I'd bet a hefty sum many of those guys don't have a father in their life. A father would say, "Get back in their son. You don't quit, you work hard and earn playing time. You don't have to play for that coach, but you can play for your team that is counting on you. Too many have gone before you that wish they could be in your shoes. It is a short season of life and if you don't quit, you will eat the fruit of your labor. Don't let that coach steal your ability to bear fruit."

But when we are not given that mindset or are held accountable to a commitment, there is no way to see other than to just walk away from a difficult situation. This book is not a cure all, but my hope is to give you a new lens in as many areas of your life so you can operate differently. **Work is sacrifice.** Work doesn't give back to you. Work takes. Work takes the most precious thing that you can never get back—time. You are going to have to work and if you think work will fill your tank so you can walk around emotionally on cloud nine, then you are mistaken. Yes, you can enjoy your work and I hope that you do, but for most we are going to have to find another path to enjoyment and fulfillment.

What I am proposing is that instead of the hope of doing meaningful work, you need to strive to find meaning in your work. Consider this: even that guy who has devoted his life to cure cancer spends most of his days failing. Each day he goes to work to doing true meaningful work – to end a particular type of cancer—and each day he only inches closer to a goal he may never reach. That guy doing meaningful work had better have something else propping him up or the sheer daily failures will remove all the wind from his sails.

Find Meaning In Your Work

Meaningful work is a myth because it is all a matter of perspective. I've had to wait on a mechanic to repair my vehicle and believe me, getting my car running again had plenty of meaning to me. Oh sure, that mechanic didn't change the world, but he sure changed mine when he went out of his way to help me get back on the road. The point is that in order to find meaning in your work, you have to serve someone other than yourself. Serving someone else always has meaning. It doesn't matter if somehow you find yourself as a stay-at-home dad while you look for work or you are assembling scaffolding at a construction site. The key to finding meaning in your work is to serve someone other than yourself. That is how you make use of the time at work beyond earning a paycheck.

If you work for a paycheck you will never be happy with work because money just won't satisfy you. I'm not telling you the way you *think* the world works, I am telling you how it really works. Money won't give your life meaning but serving people will. A mechanic can focus on fixing cars or he can focus on getting people reliable transportation. A doctor can focus on getting rid of sickness or he can focus on helping people live healthier lives. It is in the "serving people" aspect that you can find meaning in your work. By the way, serving people doesn't necessarily mean they appreciate it.

I remember when I learned this lesson. I was working as a civilian in Iraq and the civilian side of the military base got a new boss. Well, this dude was a lousy human being in my estimation, but as the someone in charge, when he tasked me with putting up some bulletin board material, I disliked him even more because I had to do it. Not only was this not anywhere near my job but it was a ridiculous waste of time . . . so I treated it as such. I did the worst job you can imagine, strictly the bare minimum. Of course, God soon reminded me that I didn't do my best and I felt God nudge me to go apologize to him and do it right. I can't fully explain what it is like to walk into a man's office that you really can't stand and know you are about to grovel. Ugh! Remember, I am a believer and one who really does love God, so when I say I couldn't stand him it means I am letting you peek behind the curtain of my heart and see I am not the Apostle Paul, let alone Jesus. Yet I went in there to explain to him that I serve God, that I didn't do my best, that I apologize, and if he didn't mind, I was going to redo that bulletin board. He smugly said "Okay" as if I just told him there was donuts in the break room. As you can imagine his response helped make the whole discussion, where my pride was shoved down my throat, almost happen in slow motion. But from that moment on, I refocused my lens and started serving that guy. He needed to see what a Christ follower looked like. My whole reason for work wasn't focused on him but I made sure that I did my job well for his benefit. My hard work may not have led to his salvation, but it gave meaning to that work and that helped me work well for him.

The reason you need to have a good view of work is because work can be toil, burdensome, weary, and life-sucking. Bosses can grind salt into that wound, and when you need the money to pay bills and have no escape, **the only way to be free is to do the work with meaning.** Many will think that doing meaningful work is what they should strive for but that is fool's gold. What does that even mean? Is meaningful work finding a cure for cancer or working with orphans? If that is the case, what do you do when you are parking cars, digging trenches, or working on an assembly line? Are those meaningLESS jobs?

See, you can't try to focus on doing meaningful work, but you must find the meaning in your work. Every job sector of society is needed. It doesn't matter if a surgeon can remove a brain tumor if the janitor can't keep the operating room clean. A soldier can't protect his post if the administrative guy doesn't ensure the ammunition makes it to the armory. Serve people and you will always have a reason to push through those tough times. Yes, you can put up with a boss because your family is counting on that paycheck, but when you can also put up with that boss so the next person on the assembly line has an easier workday, you can push through. Now, I am not saying it will be easy, but you must fight to find meaning in your work.

So once we begin fighting to view work through that lens, then what?

You probably think all that crap about showing up on time and "Having a good attitude is half the battle" is wrong, but you will find out it is pretty accurate. Be the best employee that you can be. You are replaceable in some sense but even though somebody else may be able to do that particular job, they can't hire another you. You are the only one that brings your gifts and experiences to work, but in order for your gifts to make room for you, you must be seen. Stand apart by doing more and having the best attitude instead of being the voice of complaining. It may not be at that company but eventually it will lead to something because people will speak positively about you. Do what you have to do in order to walk into work with a positive attitude. If you need a motivational speaker, listen to guys like Eric Thomas aka, the hip hop preacher, on your drive. If you need music, then listen to the music that motivates you. If you need to sing, then sing. The point is that you need to find a way to walk into work void of a negative attitude and fill that void with joy, drive, and vitality.

Let's not forget that you need to be good at what you do. A neurosurgeon does not call a plumber because he just doesn't have the time to handle his plumbing issue or because he is too good for that work. He calls a plumber because he isn't good at plumbing. And just like there are neurosurgeons that are better than others, there are good plumbers and bad plumbers. It is called hierarchy of competence. Whatever field you are in you set yourself apart by your level of competence and work ethic. It is how you create value to others. If your mom gets brain cancer, you don't just want a brain surgeon, you want the best brain surgeon you can find. The same goes for a plumber, welder, or mechanic. We want the best mechanic we can find, not the most knowledgeable but the one with the work ethic that doesn't cut corners. Believe me, those guys are out there. So be good at what you do but if you also work hard, you will set yourself apart.

And here is something for free—you will find that the more competent you are at a job, the more enjoyment you will find in your work. If everybody knows to ask you when it comes to a specific subject, it feels good. It also makes you valuable because subject matter experts are always needed.

It will take time and experience so don't expect people to respect your opinion day one on the job. You just can't bypass experience. Strive for competence but you will need time, experience, successes, and failures to become a subject matter expert. When you are just starting out nobody expects you to know much, even with a college degree. So being 22 and clueless is expected, but at 30 being incompetent isn't cute anymore.

Navigating The Workplace

Getting to where you want to be in your profession takes work and some maneuvering around people and obstacles. Working means waiting and men don't like waiting. Add the fact that we think we know best when it comes to timing and the wheels are already in motion to make mistakes. The simple point is that you will make work mistakes so don't be surprised and don't beat yourself by thinking that you should have known better. The truth is that you are just a man and men make mistakes. Men fail. Learn from failure and teach the guy behind you to watch out for the landmine. Oh sure you will hear a guy here and there say "I don't work because I love what I do." You will hear that and think that is the way it should be for you; if you could just do what you love then the work problem would be solved.

Work is hard and it will always be like that because God told Adam, "from the sweat of your brow (Genesis 3:19)." And even if you actually like what you do, that doesn't mean you will always like who you work with. That one guy is trying to make you look bad, so he gets the promotion. That incompetent boss will take credit for your work or that boss will have it out for you at every turn. If he or she was removed from the equation, work would be great. Sorry to break it to you but those are all lies and self-deceit. **You and your attitude are always the problem and the solution**, so when the people are the problem, what is the practical help I offer?

Simple—when people are the problem; do your job well. Show up on time and take it like a man. And as you do, sit with someone older and wiser and ask for their thoughts. Don't run to your buddy and ask him to tell you what you want to hear. No, get perspective. It isn't always what is said but who says it that makes it drop into your heart like a coin in a vending machine. I can remember a time when that happened for me. I was having a difficult time 'being noticed' by man or God for the work I was doing. I felt like I was going above and beyond, and it was like I was the invisible man. I asked this guy who was probably 75 at the time for his thoughts. He simply told me that one day he noticed the church grass area needed to be mowed, which happened to be about an acre and a half. He said he mowed it a couple of times just because he saw the need and pretty soon everyone just assumed he would mow it as if it was his job, so he just kept mowing. Then he said, "and that's the Christian life."

All I can tell you is when he uttered those words my perspective changed. It wasn't as if he gave me the next steps of what to do in order to be noticed, although he might have. No, in this particular case I guess God just wanted me to have a different perspective that I didn't need to be seen or rewarded; what I needed to do was serve without looking for gain. Now that doesn't mean I am telling anybody in a position where people are causing them problems to just get new perspectives, although it would help. I am saying that the answer is not within you. You don't just go to the lab and draw up pro's and con's and let that determine how you approach the situation. Each situation is different, and your intellect and experience are not enough to navigate life. You get counsel, and not from your buddies who can't stand that boss either. You seek out men whose lives attest to acquired wisdom and ask them. I'm not saying to do whatever they tell you to. I am saying that in going to them, you position yourself to hear things that will lead you to a good path or help change your perspective.

The workplace is a tricky minefield to navigate. There are times you do what wise counsel says and times when you don't. Life is not a set of right and wrong decisions but more of a lot of good, better, and best choices and you won't know which one was best until you make one and look back in time. Once you understand good, better, and best in terms of decision making when you are weighing options, you will free yourself up to fail. And when you are free to fail, then you will always feel more at peace. You need peace in your life, especially when you have a wife and children looking to you, but they need to see you succeed and fail. They need to see you succeed so you can tell them how you didn't get there on your own and need to see you fail so you can show them how to respond.

I want you to notice that time and time again in this book I will give non-answers: I don't tell you to go left or right but instead tell you to basically just pick. The reason is because there are times when life is simple; should I embezzle money from the company to pay my rent? No, you should not commit a crime in order to pay your bills. But if the question is, "Should I quit my job before I get fired because the new boss is trying to cover his mistakes?" Well, I don't know, and the truth is neither does anyone else regardless of age or wisdom. This is real life and you won't know this side of heaven so quit trying to get into the mind of God. He has not obligated Himself to tell you which pair of shoes to wear that day. Just look at your shirt, pick out a pair you think looks good with them, and go to work. If you fired for wearing ugly shoes, then understand that life isn't fair and you have to deal with it and move forward.

If your dad had been there every step of your life growing up, chances are he would have let you fail at times. Why? Simply because he knows you will be okay, but you need to learn how to fail. The workplace is a place you must learn to navigate. Do you ask for a raise? Do you tell your boss you have been working late so he knows your work ethic? Should you try to get the foreman job even though your buddy wants the job too? These questions don't have right answers and you have to learn to be okay with it. As we look at decision making, I'll try to give you a framework to think through, but you are still going to have to make a decision without knowing the outcome.

Injustice At Work

Now, with this as a backdrop what about the times when you see wrongdoing at work? In any sector a man could possibly work in, this question is an absolute beast. Do you challenge injustice or quasi-moral decisions and possibly ruin your job, career, finances, or family, or do you just keep your head down and do your job, hoping the next guy will say something? It doesn't have to be something as major as working for a chemical company that is poisoning the water of a local town. It can be as simple as an injustice where you see someone being continually overlooked for promotion due to sexism, racism, showing favoritism to friends, or just out of spite.

Let me tell you about an experience I had in my mid 30's. I was working on staff at a large church and one of my duties was keeping minutes during elder meetings. Now, my job required me to be elder-qualified and because I was respected, I was free to voice my thoughts during those meetings. In fact, my thoughts were welcomed even though I didn't have an actual vote. My approach was to really guard my voice and there were plenty of times I didn't speak even though I could have added something beneficial to the discussion. It can be tough to navigate a discussion when you're in the room but not "in" the room. But I'm telling you that at times, I could just see a better way or something missing, but because I wasn't an elder I really bit my tongue a lot since it wasn't my role.

There was a time when a guy was sought out by the leadership for an upcoming pastor/elder opening. He was told by leadership that if he wanted the job as the new Campus Pastor/Elder, it was his. This guy was a black man who was seminary trained and ran a successful ministry. and this is where it gets tricky. When the elder meeting came up to make it official, things unraveled quickly. He was being hired because a local church was giving our church their building and their older membership was going to merge into our local church. To cut to the chase, the older church was mainly older white people, and it became known that if we hired a black campus pastor/elder, they just might vote down giving up the new building.

So here is where the rubber meets the road. During the elder meeting, his race came up. All I can say is that . . . I squirmed in my chair a lot during that meeting. Now his race did come up but so did his ability to pastor and his disposition for the job. But to me, none of that other stuff mattered outside of his race because once they discussed his race I thought, that is racism at its highest form; complete ignorance. His race was actually a desirable asset regarding diversity because he would be the first black elder and the church greatly desired diversity in leadership. But when you start counting it as a negative by juxtaposing it against possibly not getting a new building, that just ain't right. One of the guys even said, "We can't miss it on this hire," meaning if we hired the wrong guy, we possibly would not get the building. I'm telling you, I cringed and cringed and cringed. I prayed and watched them struggle to do what is right; I mean, he was already told the job was his, so this discussion was supposed to be just a rubberstamp.

All the while I just hoped they would wander to the truth and give the fully qualified black man the job that he was already told was his. But there were men saying to move forward and let the chips fall where they may and others saying let's just hire him for just a pastor position and then make him campus pastor once we merge into one. Basically do a little sleight of hand; a white lie if you will.

It was a real discussion even beyond race, touching on his disposition and job background, but in the end, they made the decision to hire him on staff as a pastor and told him that at the beginning of the next year they would announce him as the new campus pastor/elder. Crisis seemingly averted. I say seemingly because sadly, even though he agreed to their hiring plan, the church leadership never made him the campus pastor/elder.

Now, let me unclearly clear—he didn't get the job because some of the elders felt they really didn't know him and wanted to see if he could really do the job first AND he didn't get the job because he was a black man, even though he was fully qualified and already promised the job. Of course as far as the public was concerned, the elders just didn't feel he was right for the position. It wasn't the whole truth but once again this is how the world works; those in power can always spin the story because they write the history books.

So before you take sides and have some opinions, don't forget who was in the room; I was. There were thirteen white men and one second-generation Mexican American. As far as I could understand, they just didn't see how their whole conversation was totally wrong for so many reasons. So why didn't I speak up you might ask. Well to be honest it wasn't for a couple of years before I knew the real answer. I was reading the Bible one morning and Proverbs 31:8-9 mentions speaking up for those that can't speak. That meeting came rushing to my mind. God put me in that room to speak up.

See, I grew up during a time when you just ignored racial ignorance. I've had well-meaning older men tell me I was a good Mexican or people say that I'm not like other Mexicans. Honestly, idiotic compliments like that happen to people all the time and like I said, I just learned to ignore them. In essence, my mind was shaped by culture instead of how God would have me engage ignorance. When God hit me with that Proverb, I immediately called that guy, by then a good friend, and apologized and said the reason his family went through such a hard time at that church was actually my fault. Those men were just ignorant and I should have spoken up. If I were the man back then that I am today, I probably would have been fired well before that day. Now don't hear me excuse their collective ignorance. Thirteen elder-qualified men who love God should be able to navigate race, buildings, and promises made without me. Now, in other areas I challenged leadership and they even though they didn't listen, it wasn't because I was silent. But I want to be clear that *my silence* during that meeting negatively affected the lives of others. Today that guy is a good friend of mine and God has a way of working those things out, but I still have the thought "What if?"

When you run across issues where your choice is to speak up or not speak up, there will be consequences, plain and simple. Either you will say something and get the full weight of those consequences, or you stay silent and the oppressed and voiceless get the full weight of your silence. Or maybe you speak up, your voice is welcomed, and the situation is rectified. Those that need to be confronted remain in ignorance, and each time you are

Regardless, speaking may cost you alone, but silence will cost you and others.

silent you give up a piece of who you are. Once you feed a stray cat, it will always come back for more and once you compromise your conscience you will find that they will always come back for more. Little by little, what was once something you would never do becomes something you do without thinking. Like I said, not every injustice is poisoning of water, racism, or sexism, but those small issues you ignore chip away at your integrity.

Practical tip—start preparing your exodus from that company when you see wrongs or injustices that you feel the need to address. Also, anytime you find yourself talking to HR, plan your exodus. HR isn't your friend; remember they work for the company. I didn't say leave, I said get your ducks in a row in case speaking up costs you your job. It is better to be a whole you and unemployed than trade your conscience for rent money. God is your provider, not your employer.

Office Politics

Once again, I can tell you about the world the way you wish it were or I can tell you how it really is. There are office politics in every sector of work and you better not consider yourself too good to play the game. Now I am not talking about cutting some guy off at the knees in order to get a promotion. I am talking about being aware of what is required to move up in your company and industry. Let me tell you how I first realized that some people were playing the game of life at a level I didn't even know existed.

Remember that I grew up not knowing how to get where I wanted to go. Well, during my senior year of high school, two of my really good friends got appointed to the

Naval Academy and West Point. It was great news that hit the school like a fresh wind of success. And you know what, I didn't even know my good friends applied, but even if I had known, I wouldn't have had the foggiest idea of how to make something like that happen. If you don't know yourself, let me tell you this: it takes an act of Congress to get appointed to one of the service academies. Remember my dad was an Air Force officer and joining the Air Force Academy probably would have been something I would had tried to do if I knew the process and how to navigate it. Well, these guys with fully engaged, college educated dads were playing chess while I was playing checkers. I basically picked a college by picking *Playboy Magazine's* number one party school . . . I didn't know how the world worked. I also didn't know I could actually be myself and succeed. Gotta be you, but ya gotta be shrewd.

If you are not careful, when you are not looking, guys will acquire skills, meet executives, play golf with management, fish with supervisors, or play cards with an influential administrator while you have your nose to the grindstone. Oh, you will be working hard and will be making a difference in the company, but that isn't all there is to navigating the workplace. Now, I am sure that some of you are thinking that I am suggesting you suck up to the boss and jump over a more qualified person for a promotion. That ain't it. I am saying that people are influenced by relationships and that translates into the need to learn to navigate those relationships. You will never outgrow the need to be good at what you do but being known for what you do by decision makers will certainly help you.

Remember when I say office politics, I am talking about having a plan to be the best you in the workplace. No matter what job you have, you will have a boss and more than likely your boss will have a boss. Wanting to one day be in the position of your boss's boss is a great thing, but you are the one that has to navigate your way to that position. You do that by knowing your work culture and arena. You do that by learning to not only navigate relationships but learning to manage relationships as well. Being a boss isn't about doing the work as much is it is about managing those that do the work. You have to be proactive in learning to navigate work relationship and you start by being aware how important they are.

Be shrewd. Navigating the corporate world requires a different set of tactics than the blue-collar world, and there are different tactics for all the different shades of professions in between. Sometimes working hard in front of the right person is more powerful than competence. Like it or not, politics is in the workplace. I don't care if you work in a church or in sales, who you know and how you play the game matters. I would love to tell you God will always counter the plans of the wicked, but for much of life He lets the tare overtake the wheat. That doesn't mean God doesn't care, it just means God is doing a whole lot more than just managing your job position, so find you contentment in him first.

God is always working, and you are acquiring skills through failure and enduring job politics. Skills advance you long-term as a person in many areas. By living through injustice, I learned to work for justice. Through that lesson in my life, I have engaged school heads, teachers, and pastors in love for the good of others. God will use those skills to work His plan.

Also another important thing to consider is your emails when it comes to office politics. *Do* keep negative emails but *never* respond in writing to negative emails. Tone is very hard to interpret so even a positive response can be viewed as negative. Something like, "I'm sorry you feel that way and I look forward to speaking in person to work things out" is about as good as you get so be careful responding. Anything on record is on record to benefit or hurt you. I'd actually recommend printing any negative emails so that you have a hard copy. Hardcopies can't be deleted and anything official like that can be passed along. I had an employer that refused to pay anyone overtime. As college students, he knew we had a great job so we wouldn't quit. Once let go, on a whim I asked the Department of Labor to help me get my overtime. They ended up investigating the company's 10-year pay record history and he wound up paying $70K in unpaid overtime. Guys were calling me and thanking me for their windfalls. But don't be proud of me; I was a horrible guy at that time and although the reason for firing me was unjust, I should have been fired for the unseen things I did. I was a great employee on paper, but God knows I was wolf in sheep's clothing.

And above all, **under no circumstance should you vent in emails.**

The point is to teach you to respect documentation and use it for your benefit because things can happen quickly and you can be blindsided no matter where you work. I know men who went into routine church meetings who walked out without jobs and one who was immediately escorted from the building. I'm not talking about being fired for incompetence or misconduct, just fired because church leadership wanted to hire someone else. If people who love God run a local church as a business, then how much more your local union job? Print those hard copies of emails well before you need them because you might not be able to access them when you do. In the military it was called covering your six (your rear position that you can't see). And to finish the thought, know what you can record in the state you work. In today's Texas, as long as one party (could be you) knows they are being recorded, you can record any conversation. I've recorded some conversations just in case. Thankfully I never needed them, but you never know. Thus you might want to check on the laws in your state.

Accomplishment

As a man, we all love the sense of accomplishment. It can be as simple as mowing the lawn and seeing how great the yard looks when we are done. There is a great feeling in completing something that points toward our own hard work, but if we place too much value on accomplishments in the workplace, we can easily deceive ourselves into thinking we are a success in all areas of our lives. Accomplishment can make an empty life look full, but you know the truth and you will lie to yourself in order to keep looking full. Here is the thing, no victory every lasts. Chasing accomplishment numbs you to the vanity of reaching a goal because you are told the victory will change everything for you. A father was meant to show you the vanity of victory. The mountaintop experience doesn't last; there is always another mountain to climb. A father helps you enjoy the process, to be present in the moment. You need to put your work in today. Be the best you can today but never think you have arrived.

Victory is found in being faithful in the mundane. You will never do something great without doing great small things nobody sees consistently. Setting work goals is good but focusing on being better today than you were the day before is how you stay grounded. Enjoy the work awards and accolades. Enjoy being the top salesman but be in the present and let the accomplishment validate what the daily work adds up to instead of it validating your existence. Accomplishment will not fill that void in your life. Putting too much value in accomplishments will breed entitlement because you feel like you earned something because of it.

Entitlement will breed laziness and you can think and operate in a way that people owe you and you don't owe them. Neither God nor the world owes you anything because of what you accomplish or what you didn't have growing up.

A quick side note about not having a head start. Some people have a head start in life, that is true. However, if you want to move forward in life then you need to put on blinders and run your own race. The phrase I use with my kids all the time is: "Don't count another man's money." That means, don't worry about him, worry about yourself. Your brother gets two donuts and you got one: don't count another man's money. Found out that your sister got a treat when she went to the grocery store with mom and you don't think it is fair? Don't count another man's money. The lesson they need to learn is that they can't live their life worrying about what somebody else has or has accomplished. They need to appreciate the things they have and put in the work to get things they want. Get to work, do your best, become a real master of your craft, trade, job, role, and you will enjoy your life more.

Look, everybody has their own sob story and no employer cares about yours. Get out there and earn respect. Get out there and earn your pay. Your boss is not accountable to you, but you are accountable to him. Don't like how he treats you? Quit. Quit whining and do your job well. Make yourself valuable and you will succeed in life. These are some over-the-top statements for sure but that doesn't make them false.

Let's get back to accomplishments: a practical tip would be to fight entitlement by never letting accomplishments have too great a place in how you see yourself. Accomplishments are great measurement tools to help you gauge how well you are working but they are not for how good you are as a person. No man will ever lay on his death bed wishing he worked to accomplish more. He won't ask God for one more day to hit his sales goal, but he will wish for more time with loved ones. I will boldly tell you to see how much you can accomplish in your job, but I will equally claim just as boldly that accomplishments are vanity. If you are already a father, you will already understand that men will always be prouder of what their children accomplish than their own accomplishments. There is more joy in being happy for others than for yourself. Be a great person, accomplish as much as you can at work, but never put any of your value in any accomplishment because it just won't last.

There isn't a Super Bowl MVP that lives every day with that mountaintop feeling. The next week, their wives still asked them to take out the trash and their kids still didn't pick up their toys. Life goes on after accomplishments and in a what-have-you-done-for-me-lately world, those awards and accolades won't save you from layoffs, cutbacks, or salary reductions if your production bottoms out.

Final Words On Work

Your family doesn't care if you are the best salesman, producer, welder, doctor, or whatever if you come home and suck at being a husband and father. Your boss and co-workers don't care if you are a great father and husband if you suck as an employee and co-worker. You have to be a well-rounded person to bless the world around you. There isn't some mystical work/life balance so don't waste your time trying to find one. There are different chapters in your life and different seasons and those times will dictate where to put your emphasis. For instance, if you are young and single, working 80 hours a week can reap some major benefits, but if you have a wife and toddlers, missing family time for work is a trade I'd never suggest you make. Your family is better off with your presence than with more money for stuff. "I wished I worked more," said no dying man ever.

Yes, be ambitious and industrious but remember hard works doesn't mean higher pay. Quarterbacks make more money than other players because the position is valued. Working smarter must be a piece of your work puzzle. I don't mean just doing your job well but creating ideas to make things better. When you share those ideas and with whom you share them adds to the soup. Be intentional to rise in the organization. When work begins to lack meaning, look for someone to help or elevate. Give and you will find you receive more. Poor financial health will be a barrier to better mental health. When you are worried about rent, food, and necessities, getting help or therapy just isn't high on your list. Thus, no matter how much you make at work, it is what you spend that will determine your financial health. Getting a raise and spending it all will keep you broke and being broke will affect your long-term mental health. What I am saying is that work is about more than pay and finding meaning; work comes home with you whether you want it to or not. Be ambitious, industrious, and shrewd, but serve others as you do.

For a few of you. You need to quit your job. Just like when you already know that the girl you have isn't for you, sometimes you know the job you have isn't for you. And just like you are scared to leave that girl because you don't want to be alone, you won't leave that job because you are afraid. You are afraid to go try what you really want to do. You are scared to start your own business, scared to change industries, or scared of the unknown. Don't let fear run your work life. God is your provider, not your employer. Take a risk and leave that comfortable job and try something else. I give you permission to fail. Quit and chase that dream. Oh, and leave that girl too . . . you are wasting her time and you're never alone as long with God in the picture.

And the final practical tip is this: when possible find someone older than you in your industry and ask them how to get where you want to go. They can tell you things you didn't even know to consider. If you are a minority try to find two men, at least one of whom is also a minority. There can be things to consider that a non-minority wouldn't know. At the same time, if you only talk to a minority in the industry you might lose key insights that only a non-minority possesses. Wisdom says if you want to rise in the workplace, ask someone who has been where you want to go. Learn from their sweat, blood, and mistakes.

CHAPTER 10

DECISIONS MAKE THE MAN

"Women and children can be careless, but not men."
—Don Corleone from *The Godfather*

That movie has so many life lessons and that quote is a great introduction to talking about decision-making. More than likely you have been careless with your decision-making but you'll never know what would have happened if you chose differently, so do yourself a favor and remove "woulda, coulda, shoulda" from your mind and embrace that failure is usually the first step towards anything great.

If you want to do yourself another favor, underline, take notes, or do whatever you can but take heed of this chapter. I contend that virtually every issue you have in your life is because of bad decisions *you* made previously. That doesn't mean it is your fault, but it does mean you are responsible. Facts.

Now don't tune out. Instead, bear down and start a habit of making good decisions from this point forward. When I am talking about decision-making, I am not narrowing in on whether you prefer Coke to Pepsi or PlayStation to Xbox. I am talking about the decisions that require more thought because of the outcome's ability to have positive or negative ramifications. In essence, decisions do three things: Allocate Resources, Solve Problems, Accomplish Goals. And as with anything, there are factors that affect our decisions. Life stage, age, level of risk aversion, current resources, how we view ourselves, and others factors all come into play when we are confronted with big decisions.

Bad Decisions

We can make bad decisions due to internal bias. Internal bias happens when our history, culture and past decisions subconsciously influence our decision making. When we have an internal bias, we are likely to forgo doing research can even subconsciously look to people who will tell us what we want to hear.

A major flaw in the decision-making of younger men is that the greatest influence in their lives are people of their own age. In most cases that means they are not gathering wise counsel but rather fishing from a pool of ignorance (not ignorance as in your friends are dumb, but ignorance because they lack the wisdom that is gained from real life experience). When we are young, we keep going to a good friend because of our internal bias and they keep giving bad information and that leads to bad decisions. It isn't that our friend is bad, he just doesn't have the best information to inform our decisions.

Another example of internal bias is when we made a decision in the past and things worked out well. We assume that it was a good decision so it becomes a part of our internal bias. I got cash on my credit card and paid my bills before and it worked out so why not just do that again this month? Recognizing internal bias can be difficult which makes getting counsel important. You may not have someone to ask, and I understand because I never had anyone either.

With the wealth of information available today on the internet we certainly have more information available. You just have to push yourself to search for different wells than you are used to drinking from. We are all aware of social media algorithms that feed us more of what we already believe. Similarly, if we just keep going to the same person or website for information, we can neglect good thoughts from other sources.

You have to be happy with truth, regardless of the source.

When it comes to internal bias and information gathering, my suggestion is to seek two or three people out with differing views when it comes to big decisions. The people you pick out when it comes to buying a house might be different from those you ask when it comes to job-related questions. The hope is not to make the perfect choice but to develop the habit of working toward making good decisions your routine rather than the anomaly.

We can also make bad decisions when today's desires outweigh the future's needs. Think back to me not changing my oil so I could have drinking money at the cost of having a working vehicle in my graduating semester.

The last reason I'll give for us making bad decisions is what we believe about ourselves. We can take too much risk or not take enough risk in our decision-making. Either we are trying to prove we are just as good as everyone else so we take bigger risks in hopes of higher rewards, or maybe we don't believe we are good enough so we don't take any risk. After all, if we fail it will only further prove we are not good enough. You have been boxed in by the world telling you what you can and can't do for so long that it has influenced how you make decisions. You can't save because there is no tomorrow for you. If you don't see your life as valuable you might take too much risk or too little.

These things are not solved overnight but if we can acknowledge we have made decisions in our past rooted in emotion, bad information, internal bias, self-image, and too much emphasis on today's wants then we can begin to move forward with making manly decisions.

What Makes A Good Decision?

Men don't make boy decisions. Wisdom gained by experience gives men the ability to make manly decisions, while a boy can only stumble upon wise decisions. **Manly decisions are rooted in three things—accountability, possible future consequences, and how those decisions affect other people.** Accountability means you take full responsibility for the consequences of your decisions. If you are not accountable you will not be held responsible for where you are today. Instead you will blame someone else and if you allow it to be someone else's fault, you won't learn. You won't learn because when you won't go back and think about what you could have done differently in your decision-making process. Instead, you will just decide that in the future that "that guy" isn't to be trusted because he caused XWZ. Being accountable is about you learning from your mistakes.

Now I must pause to say that in a large crowd there are always instances that I don't want to include when I am saying words like "fault" and "responsibility." If an adult figure preyed on your innocence and took advantage of you in a way that should not have happened, it isn't your fault. I am not talking about a child's decision that impacts today. Please understand that in this context of decision-making, I am totally excluding things in this genre. At the same time, we must consider that those traumatic events can also shape our decisions. If we don't acknowledge that, we won't seek help.

Additionally, if you are accountable in your decisions it means you make decisions that benefit not only who you represent but those your decisions affect. If you negotiate, you negotiate a win-win, not a win-lose. Now I must mention that this doesn't mean you should be a pushover who gives up his company's benefits in negotiations. I'm saying you work to find a mutual scenario in which both sides win. The point is that accountability in decision-making includes considering others as well. A take-take-take mentality often leaves you with less in life. Again, if you are not accountable you won't learn to take responsibility. Taking responsibility for decisions is absolutely man like.

Embrace the fact that your decisions affect others. A man just doesn't quit his job in a high state of emotion, because his family is depending on him. Additionally that friend at work will have extra work because you made a decision while mad. Decisions are not made rashly; they are well thought out, and that includes how the decision might affect others. That doesn't not mean that you can't make a decision that negatively impacts others, but it does mean you must make the decision with your eyes wide open. Making the decision not to join the family business might hurt their feelings but that doesn't mean you have to work there. It means that you may need to have a conversation with them, letting them know why you are choosing another path. You can't control other people's responses, but you must consider how they might respond and then ask someone how best to address them. Again, there are so many scenarios that can't be covered but no matter the situation, being a man in decision-making requires thinking beyond yourself. And once you make the decision, take full responsibility for it.

One of the most difficult things in making decisions, especially tough decisions, is considering the future consequences. It is difficult because all decisions are rooted in the fact that you can't tell the future or the myriad effects each decision will have on you and others. What happens if you choose law school over starting your own business? You won't ever know because you will never know what would have happened if you took a different fork in the road. I'll discuss making those types of decisions in just a minute but first let me bring this topic to a close.

The future consequences that can be measured or estimated have to weigh heavily on your decision. Will this decision I am about to make work toward the goal I say I want to accomplish, or will it actually set me back in another area of my life? Every time we come across a decision, we always must think of that future version of ourselves. What would future me want me to do here? Am I trading today at the expense of tomorrow?

You can't tell the future but that doesn't mean we ignore the future and say whatever will be will be. That is some sort of determinist and fatalist thinking, and it cheapens your accountability. I tell my kids all the time to, "Set yourself up for success." The reminder I want to instill in them is before they start something (make a decision), they need to stop and think in order to ensure they haven't missed something. Before making that key decision, you want to stop and at least consider which decision is better in the long run.

Our decisions must always consider the future and those affected by our decisions, and we must be accountable for our decisions.

Making Good Decisions

So how do we make better decisions? Shouldn't I just go with my gut? After all, I think I have pretty good instincts. Well, that might be true, but your instincts are usually better at helping in situations you are familiar with more than major decisions. What I mean by that is instincts can be honed with experiences. If you have been working on cars for a long time, your instincts can help you diagnose a problem after simply listening, but relying on your instincts when it comes to whether or not you should move to Seattle or stay in your current area can be disastrous. You might want to consider more information.

Of course, I am not totally discounting your instincts. I am saying your instincts are not the lone voice you should listen to in making major decisions. If you do you'll soon find out that your gut has crap for brains and more often than not, your life will suffer.

A quick note on what not to do. **Never mix emotions and decisions.** Making decisions when we are in a high emotional state will drive anyone to make a bad decision. Getting put on blast in a companywide email will certainly stir up anger and embarrassment and can easily lead to the bad decision of sending an angry email in response. Marketers leverage our emotions to make the decision to buy their products before taking the time to really think about it. They use phrases like, "Act now before we run out" or "Only 2 left' in order to create the fear that we will miss out, which drives us to buy the item right now. That bad decision driven by emotion leads to buyer's remorse. Being out $20 when we make a bad purchase isn't that bad but when make the decision to walk off the job because we are angry, we get a lot more than buyer's remorse. Furthermore, our pride will drive us to double down on emotional decisions because we don't want to admit that we were wrong. Double down on facts, not emotions.

By the way, don't think that positive emotions can't lead to bad decisions. Sometimes things just feel right but we soon find out we were wrong. When house shopping, my wife called and said she found a house and said it just felt right. When she told me how much it cost, I said, "Of course it feels right, it is outside our planned budget." When I looked at the house, I understood why it felt right. The good news in this instance is that I called a friend that manages money well and, with his insight, we decided to make an offer and ended up buying the house. And when we had to move a year and a half later, we actually ended up making money. But it is easy to see how that positive emotion could have gotten us into a house that we really couldn't afford. Side note, just because the bank gives you an amount you are approved to borrow, that doesn't mean that you can afford that much. Thank goodness we sought counsel and didn't let emotions run us.

How should one make decisions? Life is complicated but some decisions can be simplified. **If you anticipate life, you can have programmed decisions that can help in some ways.** Having general guidelines like not borrowing money, not going into debt, not spending savings, not lying to a spouse, not keeping secrets, being committed to honesty at work, only dating un-married women, always saying yes when asked for help, and on and on. Just having the rules in place not to do anything illegal, immoral, or unprofessional can simplify many decisions. For example, let's pretend you have to go car shopping and the car you really want would cause you to either dip into savings or take a car loan. Well since doing either of those is against your programmed decisions, you put that car on hold, get what you can afford, and continue to save for the car you really want.

These don't have to be immovable rules but if you take the time to outline things like this, it can simplify life. For instance, my wife and I don't loan money, we only give it. For us, if someone is in need, we would rather give the money. If they borrowed money and didn't pay it back or couldn't, it might affect the relationship. But if we give with no expectation of it being returned, we fill their need and ensure that we maintain the connection with them. Sure people have said they still want to pay us back, but in our minds we never ever care because we gave it from our hearts. Thus, we don't loan money, we only give. When there is a need, the only question is how much *should* we give.

The trouble is that life has plenty of non-programable decisions of various importance and a wide range of life consequences. You're going to make mistakes, that is just a fact of life. You can take chances when it is just you, but once you have a wife and child, you now have all their vulnerabilities laid upon you. All their needs and protection fall to you and that only adds to the pressure to get it right. But God never leaves or forsakes so us, thus never ever fear getting it wrong.

As we approach these un-programmable decisions, what should we do? First, don't place yourself in a box. **Challenge the boundaries** and constraints that naturally come to mind. Boundaries stifle creative thinking. For example, how you pay for college is a hard decision. In our current time, the primary option is to get student loans. Student loans are the natural constraint imposed on us by the times we live in and we are taught not push against it. But why not challenge that idea and find what other ways are available to you? Beyond school funding there are many situations that will arise in our life where there are boundaries and constraints that keep us from considering other ways to accomplish our goal.

If we allow ourselves the opportunity to engage our God-given creativity, we might find other ways. "Necessity is the mother of invention" is the saying we have heard before. Things were created because there was no other way to accomplish something. Too often in our decisions, we think there is no other way, so instead of engaging our creativity, we just stay within the box.

Try challenging the rules when it comes to making decisions and see if you can find additional options that you didn't have before. You might ask someone else if they can think of additional options. So many times, we don't believe we can do something because we have never seen anyone else do it. That is why we can't make decisions and never ask others. There may be people in your circle that have experiences that may inform and inspire you. When it comes to major decisions and you don't know which option to take, first challenge yourself by removing the constraints and ask again, "If neither of my options were possible, what else could I do?" That simple step can make all the difference.

The next thing you can do is **prepare to fail**. Did you know airline pilots crash all the time? You don't hear about it because it never makes the news. It isn't in the news because they fail in the simulator. Military pilots and airline pilots have been doing it for years. They basically practice failing so that when an emergency happens, it doesn't rattle them, their reactions are fine-tuned, and they remain calm. This enables them to think clearly and make good choices based in fact and not in fear.

Preparing to fail will help you conquer the fear of failure.

In the same way, don't just make a decision and hope for the best. Consider what you might do if your plans fail. What might you do? Who might you turn to if things go south? Don't place your head in the sand and say, "I'll cross that bridge when I get to it." Try to anticipate failure so you respond calmly if it happens. The military makes battle plans with every intention of succeeding, but that doesn't mean they don't have a "fall back" plan. Just like in a battle, when things happen that you couldn't plan for, you already have a plan for failure. During the pandemic, my cousin was working in medical sales and they were heavily dependent upon elective surgeries. Well when those went away, they lost most of their revenue. They had no plan and spent much of the quarantine time re-thinking their sales approach. In essence, they never planned for failure and it cost them dearly. Don't fear failure if your decision is wrong; plan for it. Of course, I'm not talking about hedging your best or giving less than 120 percent effort to Plan A. Make a decision and commit to it with everything you have. However, you can't predict the unpredictable events that might derail your plans, so have your Plan B on file.

Now, there will be times when decisions are just plain hard, when neither choice is better than the other one. It is almost like a left or right decision and there is nothing telling you which to take. Hopefully this question helps you cut through the fog. **Which decision will help me be the person I want to be?** I am not talking about which one helps you do something, I am talking about turning into your own soul where only you can truly answer the question. Too often the world, the culture, our friends, and our family have so shaped our lives that we are scared to be who we want to be. The external pressures have so influenced us that we really don't know if we are following our path or the a path we think we should be on. When things are equal, ask yourself which decision might lead you to be who you really want to be.

It might be between a decision between two women, two jobs, two cars, two bicycles, two cities, two anything. It really doesn't matter what you are deciding between; see if asking that question helps you. I sincerely hope it does.

Now in between all this, there are things like listing out pros and cons, pluses and minuses, making decision trees, and all sorts of tools to help in decision-making. **One big thing that a man needs in his toolkit when making decisions is discipline**. The sad thing is that we typically need a father to instill discipline. Kids that don't learn discipline struggle to make long-term decisions. Oh sure, some of you do but most of us must develop it on our own.

There is a trade-off when it comes to short-term and long-term decision making and it can be tricky to navigate. I remember trying to make sense of this when I was buying my first new car. It was a 1996 GMC Sierra and it was awesome. The only way I could get a car was through a friend of mine who ran a dealership. He pulled every string he could pull and got me financed at 19.6%. Yep, my credit was so bad that this was my rate, and he even had to call in a favor to get this. Regardless, there was no other way to get a car since I was broke and working at a job that paid $17K a year. With my math background, I did the calculations and even though it was a horrible long-term decision, I knew that if I gave up some short-term money I could pay off that truck early and effectively reduce that high interest rate, which is what I did. I paid that truck off in about two years and turned that seemingly bad long-term decision into a win. But believe me, it isn't something I'd ever want to do again. Robbing Peter to pay Paul will eventually bankrupt you.

The point is that you need to make decisions that help you in the long term, but there are times when you really don't have a choice except to try and turn dumb decisions into good ones. I have been there and had to dig out of the hole with discipline. Trying to figure out what to do when there is no more change in your seat cushions, nobody to call, and you can't sell your plasma for another couple of weeks is a tough spot to navigate. But even still you need to attempt to remain disciplined in your decision-making

Either you will be disciplined and make decisions that help you long term or you are going to have discipline to take dumb short-term decisions and fix them. You can't just say, "I'm going to use my tax refund to pay off debt," you actually have to do it instead of enjoying a 'well deserved' vacation. For many of you there are times where you just can't get ahead no matter what. I'm telling you that more often than not it is your lack of discipline to make the little changes that keep you behind the eight ball. Being too broke to save is a mentality, not a reality.

Discipline is about playing the long game. The tortoise beats the hare every time. You are going to make mistakes but making them when you play the game correctly will almost never set you up for pain. A famous line from the movie the Godfather is "*women and children can afford to be careless, but not men.*" Don't be careless in making decisions because you will eat the fruit of those decisions. It can either be bitter or sweet, and the choice is yours.

The hope in this chapter is to really help you understand that your choices will drive much of your daily life. You can't decide that your child doesn't getting cancer or that your boss doesn't fire you, but you will make decisions that put you in positions to respond better. Make decisions that consider the future and the impact to others, then be accountable for those decisions. Start by challenging the boundaries, preparing to fail, and being disciplined.

If you want to change your life, make better decisions. Some of you feel like you have a mountain to overcome. As I tell me kids, "How do you eat an elephant? One bite at a time."

CHAPTER 11

REPAIRING AND REBUILDING

I believe it was Malcom X who said something like the master's tools will never dismantle the master's house.

The key idea here is that there is an inherent unwillingness in a person to tear down what they themselves have built. Similarly, it is extremely difficult to tear down the structures we have built our lives on because we don't want to destroy all our hard work. We don't need to totally destroy what we have built. Instead we need to find out what parts need to be repaired, what parts need to be replaced, and what parts just need to be understood correctly. A key to helping us figure those things out is to change the way we think about our life. Part of the problem when considering our lives is that we frame our thinking like a story in a movie or book where there is a protagonist and an antagonist. Or simply put, you are the good guy in your own story or the victim or for some of you the bad guy in your own story. You can't think like because life just isn't that simple. Life is complex. There are times when you were victimized but that doesn't make you a victim for your entire life. Similarly, there are times when you were the good guy but that doesn't mean you were good your entire life. Too often, a negative experience or moment frames how we feel about ourselves. You need to change the lens you view life with so you can move forward and become the best version of yourself. Notice I didn't say you need to be better than your father or your friend. You are not competing with someone else in some way. This is a fight with yourself to be the best version of yourself.

As we approach this chapter of repairing and rebuilding, we have to first acknowledge that there are parts of our lives that are broken that need to be repaired. Well, none of those things that are broken are you. That would be too simple and actually put the focus where is doesn't belong. What has been broken isn't even our fault. We might be responsible for not making the best adjustments but that doesn't mean it is our fault. You and I should have had two loving parents that each came from two loving parents. Then that group of people should have all played their role in giving us love, security, life lessons, and all the necessary advantages to propel us forward into life.

The reality is our grandparents were probably not able to do their portion and with the removal of our fathers, our life is full of mistakes, relational issues, and emotional shortages. As we have lived our lives, other people shortchanged us, didn't see our potential, tried to help and failed, and overall added to our lives not being what they could be at this point. You and I can't cry about spilled milk; we have stuff to do.

I know what it is like to live that life and to be honest, I feel great to have missed out in many ways. Without an earthly father making earthly mistakes I feel I was spared in some ways. In the past I'd get irked when I heard some fatherless athlete describing how his life changed because a coach invested in him. Or there would be some fatherless business leader sharing how a mentor or stepfather stepped in and filled that gap. I'm like most of you; nobody ever, ever, not a coach, not a teacher, not a pastor, not a friend's father, nobody . . . nobody stopped and offered me any real help, advice, or pointers along the way. But you know what, I was never mad. I think it never made me mad because I was so prideful that I thought I could do it on my own.

But, then it hit me. God shielded me from earthly men for my own good and I believe for your good as well. There was a guy who "dated" my mom for like eleven years when I was a kid. In our little world he would be considered a godly man, but in reality that dude just used my mom, never married her, and never even took the time to be a father figure to us four kids. I'm so glad God protected me from that wolf in sheep's clothing. That guy just took from my mom's body and soul the things that satisfied himself . . . smh! Then there was that dude who sent his daughter with a note to me in high school, saying I owed him a couple hundred bucks for messing up his car. And when I gave him like $50 to start to pay it off, he sent a note back with his daughter saying he just wanted to help me realize I need to be responsible and that I didn't have to pay the rest.

Seriously, what kind of man is that? If you want to help me out, then help me out. Don't send you daughter with a note; be a man and actually teach me. Like I said, I'm glad I was shielded from learning from men who say they want to help but don't actually want to put in the work.

See, what had happened was, I was driving some friends to lunch during high school, and I whipped around him like a dumb teenage driver would and I kicked up some debris that messed up his car. Well, he just happened to be the father of the girlfriend of one of my passengers. If you knew me back then, you knew I wouldn't take it from anyone due to my arrogance. I also had an innate sense that I needed to keep my place in the herd so I could fit in and get to where I wanted to be in life, so I just shuffled and danced. But let's be real. That dude knew I didn't have a father and he didn't even have the courtesy to contact my mom about her 16-year-old boy's behavior. He didn't actually care. Instead, he used his position in the community to try and bully me while calling it help. Oh, I was a wrong for how I drove but don't tell me he was there to help me, and set a better example than sending your daughter to do your dirty work. I am glad that God saved me from "good men" trying to influence my life because in the end it benefits you.

I truly believe that God shielded me from getting any life advice from these men so that I could learn from my own mistakes and from Him. I look back and marvel at their collective silence. Remember, every one of my friends had fathers at home and yet in all those years they never said so much as, "Hey if you ever need anything, don't be afraid to ask." I truly find it a blessing because sitting here today I feel blessed and grateful that God has given me a measure of clarity for your sake. I'm not saying I've been to the mountaintop and have come down with words carved on stone tablets. What I am saying is that He has directed my life lessons, shielded me from the consequences I deserved, helped me learn without that singular father figure, and preserved my life for the good of those around me. So today my hope is to help you take steps to rebuild your life on a solid foundation.

Step 1: Start With Your Father

For many of you, there is first going to be an attempt to repair your father-son relationship as we rebuild our lives. Life is coming for us all. When you lose that job, that girlfriend betrays you, your car is repo'd, you file for bankruptcy and move back into your mom's place, that marriage ends, the children blame you . . . it is chaos. In chaos there is no direction or voice; it is total lostness. In that lostness is where you wished you had a father to tell you what do to.

In this time you will have to dig yourself out and the only way most of us can do it is by ourselves. Whether you believe it or not, there is a God who can provide that extra lift you need to get out. **God says to honor your father so it will go well with you (Ephesians 6:2).** If you want to move forward, as much as it is dependent upon you, repair your relationship with your father and God has a promise attached . . . it will go well with you.

An unseen but needed blessing comes with honoring your father regardless of his sins. Maybe it is peace, maybe it is closure, or maybe it is reconciliation but regardless of the outcome, there is a promise from God that it will go well with you if you honor that earthly father. Of course I'm not talking about bowing before him like some king; I'm just saying you have a heart that respects him because God chose him for you. Hopefully this will give you a little clarity. The Hebrew word for honor is *kabed* which translates to "weight" or "heavy." This means you just give his position the respect it deserves. There have been many a teacher I didn't like, but I sure should have treated them better because I should have honored the position a lot more.

For some of you, if you do have the opportunity to find out your family history and your father's history specifically, it may help you understand your father's failings. His mistakes were not born in a vacuum. More than likely his father failed and your father had his own hurts that you ended up paying for dearly. Learning from history is one way we learn to move forward with a forgiving heart instead of in bitterness. Regardless, repair that from your end of the bridge. You have no idea the hurt, guilt, or events of his life so take it upon yourself to make the initial steps.

Before you do though, you need to prepare yourself. Where possible give him credit where it is due. Yes, maybe your dad was harsh but consider that maybe he was like that to teach you something. Instead of being the victim, give the guy credit for trying to teach you something. I'm not telling you to excuse him for everything, but you must be open to embrace the positives that come from your painful past.

This chapter is a journey. Your story has ups and downs, funny moments and sad moments, moments that were horrible at the time but have yielded growth you would not have attained otherwise. Repairing that past relationship is to embrace that your life is worth celebrating. It is worth celebrating because you have the ability to write the ending. You have endured all that pain and you are still here. You are still standing. You should have been dead. You should have already given up. You should have been destroyed but you are still standing. You did it without him. You did it despite him. You may not be where you want to be yet, but you are moving forward. When knocked down, you got up and you will never stay down. Brothers, your life is not accidental but rather a journey that you are writing and showing that, with God, all things are possible.

You have a story to tell.

Maybe you haven't grown to appreciate it yet but that day is coming. And when it does, you will truly see that you are only the strong man you are today *because* you have been through so much. Nobody has ever done anything great without overcoming something great. The point is that you may have bent but you never broke. You may not see it in yourself and maybe nobody has noticed it in you but that special quality is in you. Just like I never had that mentor or father figure stop and tell me what they saw in me, you too missed that voice. But I am here to tell you that you are unique, loved, and you have purpose. I am telling you! You are no accident. You have withstood the pounding but you didn't break. You are still standing because *you are a man.*

So how does one try to repair a broken relationship with their father? First realize that it isn't about him but about you. You need the freedom found in letting go of his failings. You can't outrun your past so don't ignore it; deal with it head on. You are going to have to reach out, try to start over, or just let them know you forgive them. The possible outcomes are as numerous as there are fatherless men so don't walk forward with some high expectations. This is about you sweeping your side of the street so you can rebuild your life with the solid foundation that you honored your father and got God's blessing in the process. **This man is your highest offender**. Of all the people in the world, including your mother, this is the person who should have helped you and not hurt you. Even if he wasn't good at something, he could have taken you to another man for help. And yes there are those that will walk forward and give their forgiveness to an ungrateful, undeserving, unapologetic man, a man who is the direct source of much of your pain and suffering. To those men all I can say is ain't nothing you can do but turn around and release that evil man to God's wrath. So forgive and as Romans 12:19 says, leave room for God to be vengeful.

Hopefully many of you have a father that was not a monster but just not a good father. Maybe there is the possibility of not just honoring his title but building a relationship. Just take the first steps in getting to know him. If he still is not emotionally available to this day you can just ask questions that don't require emotions. Ask questions even when you know the answer. If you are thinking about buying a car, just ask him what he thinks about the car and how you plan to pay for it. What is something you wish you had never done? What would you tell your younger self? Biggest mistake? What was your dream job growing up? Dream car? What female movie star did you love as a kid? Where have you always wanted to visit? These types of questions are not about answers but about him learning to communicate with you. It is about asking him practical questions to help develop a relationship that might grow roots. A relationship isn't built in an event but rather in the everyday.

If you have positive memories, write him a Father's Day letter that recounts a positive memory that you had of him, something that really made a difference in your life. If you are good with your hands, make him something. If he likes sports, take him to a game. This whole chapter isn't about reconciling a broken relationship, although that would be great. This chapter is about finding ways to honor what God has given you.

I used to meet with a college guy whose father was a fundamentalist-type who believed alcohol was pure evil. The dad wasn't a bad father and in fact, paid for this guy's private Christian college education and was very involved his son's life. What was amazing was that when this college guy turned 21, he could legally drink alcohol yet he decided not to do it. He met with his dad and told him that although he could legally drink, he chose not to drink because his dad was paying for his school and alcohol was something his dad loathed. See totally on his own, not with my direction but totally on his own, he honored his father. It isn't about the action but about the heart. This guy looked for a way to honor the father who was paying for his school. I can't tell you exactly how this young guy was blessed by God but I can tell you God fulfills his promises.

The only way to do that is to by being the bigger man. Being the bigger man is who you want to be in life, so starting with the man whose DNA you share makes sense. You can't go back and relive the past and I certainly don't promise that you will gain the father figure you have always needed. What I do know is that if you honor him, you know that God promises it will go well with you.

Of course there are a handful of you that can't reach out to him. Maybe he passed or maybe you are adopted and that information is something you will never know. That's ok, my boys are adopted and some will never know their biological father. This will be something they do between God and themselves. There won't be closure, there will only be finding a peace with God's ways. At some point everyone will experience what it is like to pray and know that God leaves somethings unanswered. For some of you men, just make sure you actually bring it before the Lord. Tell him all that is in your heart; He knows it anyway.

There is only one generation the Lord honors. The elders. The gray hair. Everything flows from the top down so as much as it is dependent upon you, repair that relationship with your father. At the minimum, forgive him.

Step 2: Start Rebuilding

Next, be intentional about giving what you didn't get. Be an encourager to those around you. It may sound out of place with rebuilding your life, but the practical begins with how you see things. To be an encourager, you have to learn to be grateful for what you have, not always focus on what is missing. Looking for ways to encourage people around you means that you have to look on the bright side when they can't see it. You will call them to do the things they think they can't do and to try things they are afraid to try. One of the things a father does is create a safe place for failure. It builds security in a child. When you are the one that looks to lift others up and go beyond what they think they can do, it changes you. And beyond it changing you, you will find that you will end up getting that same type of encouragement from others. In a physical *and* spiritual sense, you reap what you sow. I'm not talking some mystical "law of attraction" mumbo jumbo; I'm telling you that it is right and good for you to be grateful for what you have and use that lens as a catalyst for encouraging others. Don't hear me say to encourage others to be grateful. Encourage others as a father encourages his son when teaching them to ride a bike. A father knows that it is scary but if they keep trying, their body will learn to balance themselves and they will be able to ride without training wheels. Once those training wheels are off, there is no bigger smile than when a child is riding on their own. Be that encouraging person that pushes people beyond what they think they can do!

While you are giving what you didn't get, also push yourself to understand what others feel. It is called empathy. Rebuilding your life using empathy will help you stop and listen in order to gain understanding. I expect my 5-year-old to make 5-year-old mistakes because he is 5. When he makes a mistake I automatically empathize, give grace, and help him learn so that he won't continue to make that mistake again when he is 7. Too often when people do or say things, we automatically assume that we understand the "why" behind what they said and react strongly, whether positively or negatively. Great customer service representatives are naturally empathetic. They endure aggravated customers who speak harshly because they understand that the person is mad at what they are going through and don't take it personally. That frees them up to actually help solve the problem.

Trying to understand why people say and do things will positively impact your life in big ways. Empathy is one of the most powerful tools for becoming a better version of yourself. People everywhere are broken and operating every day from that brokenness. That means that their interactions with you and those around them have the potential for misunderstanding and conflict. Deploying empathy into any interactions puts you on the path toward understanding. Understanding will automatically cut through your uninformed reactions and help you connect with that person. The more and more you deploy empathy you will find that more and more people around you are not your enemy but rather people that need to rebuild their own lives.

And the last couple of things I want you to do are practical and can't be not done in a moment. **See yourself differently**. One of the most special things you will realize is that no matter who is in it, a school picture of a kid brings joy. When you look at a picture of a 2nd grader all you see is fun, possibility, innocence, potential, and all things good. There is the smile that missing teeth brings. There is nothing but positive. But when you look in the mirror, do you see those same things? Do you see potential or wasted time, failure, pain, loser, depression, and sadness? Well, when you look in the mirror, I need you to see the same potential staring back at you as when you were in the 2nd grade. Life isn't over, you have more in front of you, and you are writing that part of your life. You must, must see yourself differently. I am absolutely positive there is potential in you that you have not yet tapped into yet. If you keep yourself in the box that you and others have placed you in, you will limit what you can accomplish. If you wait until you "do something," you probably won't ever do what your actually capable of.

I'm not talking "fake it 'till you make it." I am saying that you can't measure what is in you because you don't know what you are capable of doing. If you have ever done a confidence course full of obstacles and challenges that push you to do what you didn't think you could do and challenge you to do it as fast as you can, then you know it is a challenge of you against you. That is life: you vs. you. If you approach life as a competition with other people you will never measure up because nobody stays on the mountaintop. Records are made to be broken and a new champion will eventually be crowned. You have to see how much is in you and to do that you have to see potential looking back at you in the mirror, not the sum of your mistakes.

So how do you measure success? You can't concern yourself with that, instead you really have to grasp that you are never a finished product. There is more in you than you realize. There are dreams you have not even dreamed because you have not experienced enough yet. Having a wife, kids, and grandkids will all reveal things about yourself you didn't even realize were in you.

And lastly, if at all possible, do some sort of counseling. I don't care if it is AA, Celebrate Recovery, biblical counseling, or seeing a trauma counselor. **You have to name it to tame**

it. The only way to be free from emotional wounds is to identify them so you can put them behind you. Working in a counseling environment will help you name it so it can be tamed, closing that chapter forever. For my black brothers out there, a friend of mine wrote *Permission To Be Black—My Journey With Jay-Z and Jesus.* In essence, a man with enough street cred to spare lets down his guard and shares his life in hopes of helping others live free from their hurts. Regardless of what you do with this book, I fully believe that all people are broken and in need of outside help. The book I mentioned earlier, *The Body Keeps Score*, has all the science. Do yourself a favor and find a way to name it so you can tame it.

My brother, you must realize that if you will do your best to repair what is behind you, you can move forward and built the path in front of you. Then you can fully expect that those who follow you will be better off because you ended one cycle and started a new one. Repairing and rebuilding is not only about your own joy but also about the joy of those close to you. It is the city on a hill that can't be hidden. If you don't make the climb to the top of the hill, how can you be a part of the city that blesses many? Your greatest joys will come when helping others and you will help more people the happier you are with who you are.

Pro tip—**Listen more than you talk. I'll say it again: Listen more than you talk.**

CHAPTER 12

ONE LIFE: LEAVE A PATH NOT A LEGACY

It is easier to build strong children than to repair broken men.

—Frederick Douglass

Brother . . . everybody has a sob story and life is hard. You can't afford to take the easy way anymore. Taking time to escape and smoke weed, get lost in alcohol, chase pleasure, or wander without a defined direction are not paths that bear fruit. Your father was not around to tell you that life is hard and there are times when you won't have the will to go on but you *can* do it. There is more in you than you think; just don't quit and you it will rise up from within. And after those moments that you failed and quit, he was not there to tell you, "It is okay. Just get up and try again."

But in the words of Rocky Balboa, "It is about how much you can take and keep moving forward." You will get the wind knocked out of you. Somebody close will betray you. Someone will die. A spouse will cheat. You will put all your eggs in one basket and it will all unravel. You will fund your big idea and lose it all. That child you raised right will follow that wrong path. Life is hard. . . .

But there is much life in front of you and you can rebuild with less than nothing. God created everything out of nothing and He can rebuild your life out of your failures. Countless drug addicts have become drug counselors and countless successes have been born out of countless failures. The shoulda woulda coulda game is for those that only look through the rearview mirror. Failure is the greatest teacher if you will keep trying. Just get up, son, and you will be more than you thought you could be. Time to rise and grind.

So look man, we have to talk about leaving more than a mark, more than legacy. A legacy is about your name living on in what you have accomplished. A legacy points to you. A legacy seems like something to strive for, but a legacy isn't the deep end of the pool. If you want to be more than you thought possible then do more than you thought possible. Instead of thinking of leaving your mark on this world via your legacy, I want you to get up, finish your race, and **leave a path for others to travel in hopes that they go further than you**. Even if you can't finish the path, you do everything you can to make it

leave a path for others to travel in hopes that they go further than you

easier for those that follow after you. Maybe all the fathers that went before you didn't leave you a path but you leaving a path is about ending that cycle and starting a new one. It is gonna require work and you can't fear failure.

To really leave a path that others can follow, you really have to embrace change. Change is hard to embrace because we are already comfortable with who we are. Do not be afraid to lose who you think you are; imagine what you can become if you embrace change. You have already started making changes. That is why you picked up this book. Now let me be clear: you might not be the person that enjoys the fruit of your work, but you can be the one who creates possibilities for generations to follow. You may live a life in debt and live paycheck to paycheck up to the day you die, but you can also teach your kids that you are in the place you are because of your poor decisions, and if they listen, they will never be in the same spot.

Leave a path. Teach your kids how to see so they can navigate life with fewer stumbles. Situations will change but the lens of life will adapt to any situations. My kids have to learn to navigate the world on their own, but there are phrases that I constantly say that hopefully stick in their minds and illuminate their path. Each phrase just reinforces basic lessons that will help them in their daily live. Here are some of them. I hope they help you as well.

Things I constantly say and the lesson:

Things take longer than they take—plan for delays

Use things for how they are made—Don't create your own problems by misusing something

There is a way God made things to work—Don't work counter to God's design

That's why you wear shoes—protect your feet

Safety first; mission always—Safety is not an option

Don't count another man's money—Be happy with what you have

Wants vs. Needs—prioritize things

Set yourself up for success—plan before you start something

Laziness gets you more work—Do things right the first time

Worry about yourself—All you can control is your own action or reaction

These phrases were not handed down to me, these are things I picked up along the way that will benefit them in every stage and area of life.

In the song The Story of O.J., Jay-Z attempts to give young listeners valuable life lessons from all his experiences. They need to see life through a long-term lens, and they will be better off for it. There is so much to say about that particular rap and I wish I copyright law would allow me to print some of the lyrics. I encourage you to find wisdom where it lies, use it, and pass it along. The reason I bring the song up is because I too wish younger men would learn from my experiences and learn to play the long game.

You're not going to overcome the effects of fatherlessness in your life by reading a book or following some simple 3-step program. You are going to do it by unlearning your current ways of thinking, embracing new ways of thinking, letting God bring new people into your life, and being open to actually becoming who you were created to be. Then you will begin to be the fulcrum point that changes the future generations that follow. You have to strive to be content to be happy that *you* made it possible for others to walk into a land that you bought, cleaned up, tilled, fertilized, and sewed in. Knowing God is knowing the One who makes it rain and grows the crops. Those after you might reap and enjoy the harvest that you worked so hard for.

I can't stress enough that the greatest thing you can do it leave a path. A video I routinely share is one of a Japanese sword maker[14]. His great desire is to create a sword on par with the ancient sword makers, but more than that, he desires his disciple to go beyond him. This sounds an awful lot like Jesus in John 14:12. This is who you need to be—great, but wanting greater things for those who follow. Do yourself a favor and look up the video on YouTube.

Many a CEO or leader have accomplished "great" things and left a legacy or mark, but they also sacrificed their family in order to do it. You have to try to do great things while considering the impact you have on others. You don't live in a vacuum and your actions and decisions have consequences outside of yourself. You have to make changes to yourself for you and for others. That means you are going to have to figure out how to do it, and that takes wisdom.

I always encourage anyone seeking wisdom to make it a habit to read the book of Proverbs often. You didn't have

---

14. YouTube—The Sword Maker—Korehira Watan, one of Japan's last remaining Swordsmiths (The Documentary Network) published Jan 8, 2013

a wise father. This is what Proverbs is for. Over and over, "Listen to me son" is a phrase that is used. This is an open letter to you to help you learn wisdom.

Now I can't define what leaving a path is because we are all different. It can be as simple as a college fund or as complex as being there every step of the way for your infant child. It isn't the exact path that is important. It is that you want more for your family tree than for yourself. End the cycle. Be the change.

One Life

Leave a path but you also remember that you only have ONE LIFE . . . you need to enjoy your life. **You only have one life, so go for it.** Enjoy the ride!! Start that business. Reach for that dream. Step out from the shadow of who they told you that you are. If you are young and single, take big risks when you want. If you are married with responsibilities, sell her your vision and take a calculated risk together. Regret leaves a mark on the soul; don't give it a foothold in your life. This is your life, leave that path for others to follow but you have to have fun while doing it or you will finish tired and angry. Your great grandchildren may benefit from the path you leave but they will never truly appreciate it. Have fun and even if you end up only leaving signs that say, "Do not enter," it will help them go farther. Hopefully my life of mistakes gives you a leg up on life. Sadly most of my "Do not enter" signs are from times when I thought I was having fun but are now regrets. Regrets because I wasted time. Time is something you can't get back. My college years were a lot of fun and full of excess, but that is not the fun that gives back. That fun is empty and doesn't last.

As a Steelers fan, I can't stand Tom Brady but when he was down 28-3 in the Super Bowl, that dude was still enjoying the game. I don't care what kind of hole you are in; you can still enjoy life as you make your comeback. Life is a journey so enjoy your life and seek to enjoy the process of changing your life. Yes, save some money but don't forget to get a double scoop of fun whenever possible.

My fun is traveling, meeting people, starting a business, deciding to write books, and so many other things in the last 20 years. And looking forward, my dreams are still developing. I'd love to live in Israel; there is a master's degree program I have great interest in. I'd love to enter state government and make some changes for the better. I'd love to be a part of starting a church that operates totally different than most churches in America. So many things I want to learn, do, and experience, and none of them involves a keg party and single women. Growing up means leaving childish thing behind but growing up does not mean leaving fun behind. Growing up means never selling yourself short. Go do those things you want to do. Enjoying life isn't for the rich and famous; enjoying life is for those who won't settle for less. Pain will come to all but even pain isn't understood without the feeling of pleasure. Have fun growing, making new decisions, digging out of the financial hole you are in, failing, starting over and on and on. Get bacon on that unhealthy burger and two scoops of your favorite ice cream because you only have one life to enjoy.

Remember, you are the end of one cycle and the beginning of family line that can impact generations. You have one life, that is it. You don't get to re-do mistakes once you make them. You owe it to yourself to have the best life possible. It doesn't matter if you grew up with the best father ever or you grew up in the foster care system, you can have a life you enjoy and are proud of. You can disagree with me when it comes to money, decision-making, and other areas of this book but you can't argue the fact that if you are willing to change, you still need other people. Fun is best when shared. Get a good wife, make some good friends, do crazy things. Never stop learning.

I can't say it enough, you only have one life. Enjoy it and make things better for those coming behind you. The further you get down the road, the more fun you can have along the way. And at the same time, the further you get down the road the clearer the path it is for those behind you. You have gone through too much to just get by living paycheck to paycheck or going into debt just to have fun. You are not owed anything from anyone, but you do owe you. You deserve to come out on the other side smelling like a rose, but nobody is going to give you anything.

You are the end of only cycle and the beginning of a cycle nobody in your family ever knew was possible.

You are going to have to change the way you see yourself, others around you, and how to live life. You just have to start by believing.

Head To A Mirror And Tell Yourself The Truth

As I look in the mirror, I see beauty; not handsome but the beauty of creation. I am chosen. God made

> me and gave me what is good. Fallen men have distorted the image in me but today I forsake their teachings of who I am, and I receive what God says about me. I am not just a male, I am a man. I look in the mirror and I believe. I believe. I am a glorious son of God. God delights in me. People may forsake me, but He will never leave me. God's love for me is full today. I don't have to be better; He loves me in fullness today. I receive that love in Yeshua's name.

As I finish this chapter, I know many of you are like me and didn't have a pet name given to them by your father; Baby Boy, Honey Bear, Sam I Am, Fat Man, Little Dog, Little Bear. As far as I know, I never had one of those, but I like to think that one day, my Heavenly Father won't just say, "Well done good and faithful servant" but instead will say, "Well done __________, you are a good and faithful servant." And in that space I will hear that special name He has just for me. If you a follower of Jesus, know that there is One who loves you and has been watching out for you since before you were born. He has a name for you that only he knows . . . keep following and you too will hear, "Well done _________!" Whatever name fills that space, know that you might be fatherless in this world, but you have never been without THE FATHER.

THE END

EPILOGUE

Godly Character Isn't Built In A Day

I grew up in a charismatic church and it wasn't until much later in life that I really appreciated the power of letting the Bible shape me. You can have a real love for God, a desire to follow Him, and a great plan, but everybody has a plan until they get punched in the mouth (by sin). This really isn't a chapter but a footnote that will bring more radical change in your life than any other practical tip. Meditate on Scriptures intentionally so they can transform you from the inside. *Living By The Book* by Howard Hendricks will help you learn to meditate on Scripture and to be honest, if you have not read it, I would make it your number one priority. I had a very sketchy sexual past but once I started running after God hard, I changed drastically. I didn't kiss my wife until our wedding and it wasn't because of some holier than thou legalistic reason. I didn't kiss her because 1 Corinthians 6 and 7 changed me. I read and re-read those chapters and then one day it just struck my heart that my body is not mine. So in chapter 6, God let me know that my body is not mine when I was single and chapter 7 tells me that even after marriage my body is not mine. This wasn't some simple reading of words; I truly felt that I could not give away my body before we got married.

Oh I have known plenty of guys who had all kinds of physical boundaries and rules with their girlfriends or fiancés, and all of their boundaries just couldn't hold up. I had one friend that had to start doing their pre-marital counseling homework in public because they just couldn't keep their hands off each other. And I am not talking some JV Christian; this brother was a beast. But what's a brother gonna do when he and the woman he loves and desires are in a room alone together? Best intention boundaries fade every time.

So what is my point? That I am awesome because I waited? Of course not, my point is that spiritual transformation from the inside is life-changing. I once heard a preacher mentioned a pre-marital counseling session with a young guy where he asked what God said about marriage. The young man said, 'duuuhhh' and the pastor said, "You mean you are getting married and you don't know what God says about marriage?" I was single at the time and there is no way I wanted to end up feeling dumb like that young guy. So not knowing the answer myself, I went to the reference section of my bible, looked up marriage, and started studying those passages. I can tell you the practice of meditating on passages of scripture and really studying them really helped me grow and overcome issues in my life. It is one thing to have a plan and it is another to have a plan and be empowered to walk it out.

When given the opportunity, I tell young people that when asked about particular areas of life, they should have an answer to what scriptures shaped that area of their life. For instance, is it okay to drink alcohol? Well, if they are under 21 the answer should not be one related to alcohol. The verse should be Romans 13:1-4 because before they are 21 it isn't even legal. Once they are 21, *then* they can answer the alcohol question but before then, if Romans 13 has shaped their hearts, it won't even be a decision.

Here are just a few scriptures that you can meditate on and begin shaping different areas of life. Again, don't just try to memorize them; meditate on them.

Money—2 Corinthians 9:6-7, Hebrews 13:5, Proverbs 22:7, 1 Timothy 6:10
Work—1 Corinthians 10:31, Colossians 3:23
Fear—Psalm 27, Psalm 56:3-4, Psalm 23
Uncertain times—Proverbs 3:5-7, Isaiah 30:21
Sex—1 Corinthians 6 and 7, Colossians 3:1-8
Female Relationships—1 Timothy 5:2, 1 Thessalonians 4:3-5
Friends—1 Corinthians 15:33, Proverbs 18:24
Marriage—Ephesians 5:25, 1 Peter 3:7
Social Media—1 Peter 3:8-13
Anxiety—Matthew 6: 25-34, John 14:27

NUGGETS

God Doesn't Waste Time

Would you spend the month of April (with no sleep) on social media? Well, if you average two hours a day on social media, you will have spent a whole thirty days of this year on social media.

The good news is that no matter what your life has consisted of to this point in your life, God hasn't wasted a nanosecond of His time. His handiwork goes on behind the scenes whether you are an active participant or not. I distinctly remember the end of my 8th grade year when Mrs. Penland, my math teacher, told me that she was placing me in 9th grade Algebra, not Pre-Algebra. My friends were all going to be in Pre-Algebra and I argued with her that I didn't care about being in Algebra, I would rather be in Pre-Algebra. Well, she totally ignored me and placed me in Algebra, and the next year, not only did I still not care about being in Algebra, I could not stand my Algebra teacher.

But her one decision changed the course of my life. When I changed schools in the 10 grade I was in Geometry not Algebra and that group of smart, affluent kids put me onto a college path I never knew I needed to be on. Being in the same classes with them eventually led to being in honors classes along with them as well. I discovered my path out of small-town USA was going to be laid by letting my schoolwork lead the way. See, Mrs. Penland was working for God and she didn't even know it. He knew the path I needed to be on and He ensured I got what was best. I didn't need my friends or to learn higher math; what I needed was to be around different people to change my worldview.

Or another instance of God not wasting time was when I was broke, jobless, directionless, and angry because I was doing my best to follow Him. There I was on my knees yelling at God for answers. "You took my father so that means You need to help me! I need help! If I had a son, I would help him. I wouldn't just be silent. Even if I couldn't help him, I'd pick up the phone. I wouldn't just watch him suffer. Answer me, God! Answer me! You're God and your supposed to be a father to the fatherless so why don't You help? Just tell me what to do!" On and on I went, screaming, crying, and utterly lost looking for answers. Eventually I was so tired from yelling that I ended up just laying down, saying I'm sorry and that I knew He is God and He knows better than me, even though I really didn't understand what that meant. But almost twenty years later and with five kids, I know that there too will be times when I'll have to let my own kids learn hard things. They have to learn to navigate life without me.

Giving some answers can rob someone of the experience that will teach a deeper lesson. Not picking up a crying child can also be a lesson to them that they can get up by themselves. God isn't going to rescue me from life, He is preparing me for it. I am glad I never got many of the things I dreamed of at 18 and certainly glad I didn't get the woman I wanted at 18 either. God doesn't waste time. That time where

God wasn't answering me was a lesson. It is a lesson I have learned and continue to learn. The lesson is that I don't have a "destiny." Destiny assumes some sort of destination. Life is a process and God doesn't waste time. Even those moments where you have nothing but questions and get no answers, you are still growing. You are never standing still even when you are standing still; He is moving the ground underneath you. You are never complete, you never arrive, and you are not done until you breathe your last.

Health

No matter how athletic you are, you can't outrun your fork. You are a physical and spiritual being and the younger you are the more likely you are to take things for granted. I hope that you take care of your mind and body so that you can live a long, full life. You need to have a healthy relationship with food, and if you need help, the bookstores are filled with books about healthy eating. Don't hear me encouraging you to find the right diet to lose weight. Health is about enjoying life without self-inflicted medical issues. I am saying you need to be proactive have a healthy relationship with food.

You will also need to learn to take a break from life. Creativity flows from a quiet mind. Being away in whatever way refreshes you, will allow your mind to discover ways to move forward in life. A key to finding stillness for some, is to be active in some way. They may run, build something, or do something methodical that requires focus. I have five kids and don't get a lot of me time to really have a hobby, but about a year ago we did a family puzzle and I found that while doing it by myself, I lost all thoughts except finding the next puzzle piece. Now, my normal relaxation is going to a movie theater by myself, but it was interesting to find mental relaxation in another unexpected form. So whether it is being active, being still or do something with your hands, find a way to rejuvenate yourself.

Sleep is one-third of your life. That means if you are 24 years old, you have already spent eight years of your life sleeping. Yeah, that is a long time. Make the most of your sleep. Get a good mattress and make your room comfortable. I tell my kids there are really only three things that can happen when we sleep: the enemy can disturb our sleep, God can speak to us, or we can just sleep. Maybe we get good rest or maybe we don't. I'd rather God speak to me and get a peaceful night's sleep. So every night we invite God to speak to us, ask God to protect us from the enemy's attacks, and ask God for peaceful rest. This isn't some check-the-box prayer at the end of the night. I truly want this one-third of their lives to be fruitful, so why not invite the God who doesn't sleep or slumber into that part of their lives? My suggestion is that if you are not doing it already, then definitely start inviting God into that part of your life. I'm sure many of you have had interrupted sleep over the years and this simple change will benefit you from day one.

Pornography

It is easy to just tie yourself to what today's world calls it—an addiction. That weakens belief because you are giving excuses. The spirit is willing, but the flesh is weak. There is a physiological event that likens itself to addiction, but the core is the same—you like sin. You like pleasuring yourself.

You are your own god and you please yourself. Women, even the image of them, are there to serve you and your desires. Saying you have issues with lust leaves the beast in the dark. If you have been looking at porn for any length of time, it has perverted or grown. Nobody begins with kiddie porn. That dark place began with simple lust of the flesh that has grown out of control. When you talk with whoever it is that you trust, you need to be specific about what you are looking at and for how long. Saying lust keeps your sin in the same realm with everyone's general sin, but this is not the full story.

So what is the practical? You have spiritual and physical problems, and they must be tackled together. The physical pleasure that your body and mind desire is the addiction most speak of. However, the spirit is greater and can overpower and even transform your physical needs. It will take some work with a biblical counselor or in a program like Celebrate Recovery in order for you to grow. There is a wrong belief about God that you are holding onto that needs to be let go. Your body is screaming that it needs that whole process of pleasure again and you really don't believe that God's ways are best, and therefore you don't possess the spiritual power to overcome that desire. That is why Paul says, "I beat my body into submission" (1 Corinthians 9:27). The flesh must be overcome by the spirit, and that isn't something that is accomplished overnight. There are some great books out there like *At The Altar of Sexual Idolatry* by Steve Gallagher, and I highly encourage you to pick one of them up, but a book alone will not fix you.

That means opening up to a counselor, trusted friend, or pastor. Typically, men will take the label "addiction" and use that as an excuse for a lifelong battle which allows them to keep stumbling. If you are a believer, you have the power that raised Christ from the dead living in you. You can't tell me that the Spirit of the living God is not greater than your addiction. Don't hear me say that, for some, it will not be monumentally more difficult than it will be for others, because that isn't a true statement. Some will have to battle and resist to the point of shedding blood (Hebrews 12:4), but it is possible to put it so far into your past that it becomes a faint memory. This is just a short section because the actual subject would take a book to explain, but I needed to bring it up because mastering your flesh is part of being a man. If you don't, it will spill over into other areas of your life. Some will no longer engage in sex with their wives because all their sexual energy is spent on porn. Others will use their wives as tools for masturbation instead of approaching sex as a union, two becoming one. It is not uncommon for single men to have a problem with masturbation and when the get married, instead of masturbating, they just use sex with their wives as a "legal" means of pleasuring themselves. Their wives are solely instruments for them to use for personal pleasure rather than mutual enjoyment. Porn is a monster, and you must master your body lest it wreak havoc on your life.

You must drag your actual sins into the light in order to get help.

Look, like I said, this is a subject that is a book in and of itself. It isn't possible to tackle it all head on, but this book is meant to be as practical as possible for men without a father. If you have a history of porn issues or you are currently beginning to struggle, here is the plan. Say the words, "The Holy Spirit is more powerful than my flesh and I am so loved that I don't have to do better before coming to God for help." Next, after you say that, pray and ask God where you should go next for help. Is it a counseling ministry or pastor? Either way, it must be revealed in its' worst form if you want to be free. As long as a portion of it is in darkness, it will have power over you. If you are married, your wife probably doesn't need to know the details, but somebody should. Whatever you do, just don't lie to yourself and give yourself an excuse to disbelieve that through God, this sin isn't totally conquerable. You are more than a conqueror (Romans 8).

Wall of Manhood

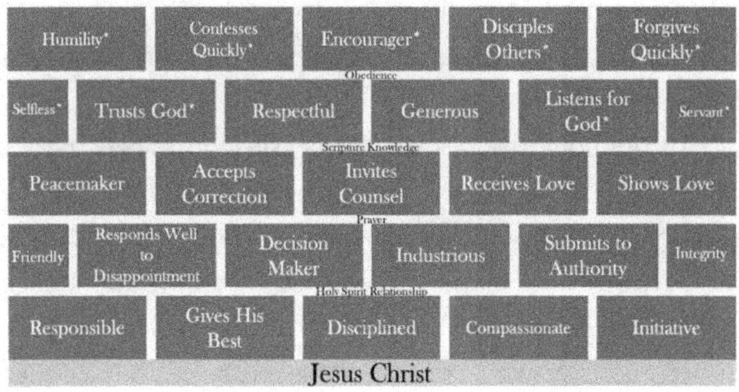

1. Responsible
2. Gives His Best
3. Disciplined
4. Compassionate
5. Initiative
6. Friendly
7. Responds Well To Disappointment
8. Decision Maker
9. Industrious
10. Submits To Authority
11. Integrity
12. Peace Maker
13. Accepts Correction
14. Invites Counsel
15. Receives Love
16. Shows Love
17. **Selfless**
18. **Trusts God**
19. Respectful
20. Generous
21. **Listens For God**
22. **Servant**
23. **Humility**
24. **Confesses Quickly**
25. **Encourager**
26. **Disciples Others**
27. **Forgives Quickly**

The Wall Of Manhood would take an entire book to describe, but I believe this visual will be useful for many of you. It is something I created so my sons would know these are the traits they need to portray consistently in order for me to consider them to be men. Men are built little by little, brick by brick, so I expect it to take time for them to possess these traits consistently.

Throughout the years I have asked guys when they became a man or when their father considered them to be men. Nobody ever had a solid answer. I decided to have a standard my boys could strive for so they have no doubts. I am here to help them but the sooner they put in the work to become men who embody these traits, the sooner they become men. There are two categories: traits that every man should possess, and additional traits God requires of men. The foundations of my four sons needs to be Jesus Christ and the mortar that will hold their lives together will be their relationship with the Spirit of God, prayer, scripture knowledge, and their obedience to the Father.

I truly hope this gives many of you something to strive for and that possess and live these traits out daily.

RESOURCES

Websites

Association of Biblical Counselor (www.christiancounseling.com)

Association of Certified Biblical Counselors (www.biblicalcounseling.com)

Celebrate Recovery (www.celebraterecovery.com)

Kahn Academy (www.khanacademy.org/college-careers-more/personal-finance)

Financial Peace University (www.financialpeace.com)

Crown Financial (www.crown.org)

A Guide To New Testament Giving by Jim McClarty

www.salvationbygrace.org/wp-content/uploads/2014/12/grace_giving.pdf

Books

The Body Keeps the Score: Brain, Mind and Body in the Healing of Trauma by Bessel van der Kolk M.D.

At The Altar of Sexual Idolatry by Steve Gallagher

Clever Girl Finance by Bola Solunbi

This Momentary Marriage by John Piper

Permission To Be Black – My Life With Jay-Z and Jesus by Adam Thomason

Debt Free Degree by Anthony O'Neal

The Total Money Makeover by Dave Ramsey

Rich Dad Poor Dad by Robert Kiyosaki

Never Split The Difference – Chris Voss

Living By The Book – Howard Hendricks

The Gospel Advent Book
CHRIS CHAVEZ
SARAH DAMOFF

A FOREVER FAMILY FOR ANTONIO
A GOSPEL ADOPTION JOURNEY
STORY BY CHRIS CHAVEZ • ILLUSTRATED BY MICHAEL BROWN

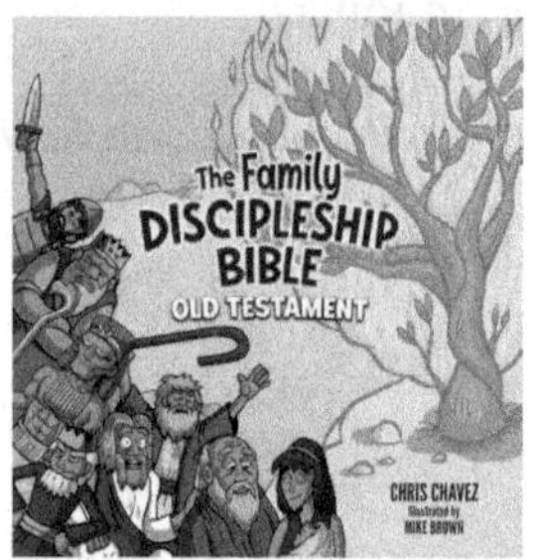
The Family DISCIPLESHIP BIBLE
OLD TESTAMENT
CHRIS CHAVEZ

LA BIBLIA del Discipulado para la Familia
ANTIGUO TESTAMENTO
CHRIS CHAVEZ

The Family DISCIPLESHIP BIBLE
NEW TESTAMENT
CHRIS CHAVEZ

LA BIBLIA del Discipulado para la Familia
NUEVO TESTAMENTO
CHRIS CHAVEZ

ABOUT THE AUTHOR

Chris Chavez has been married to Heather for twelve years. They have twice adopted siblings from the foster care system: Antonio, Moriah, Samuel, Thaddeus and JJ. After the childhood death of Chris' father, God has turned that experience into an opportunity to help others grow in their faith. Chris has previously published 5 books including *The Family Discipleship Bible Old Testament* and *New Testament.* In addition to writing, he has served in various pastoral roles and as an elder during his time in ministry. He is currently writing additional books to equip believers. Chris and his wife own and operate a window covering company in Katy, Texas.

www.ingramcontent.com/pod-product-compliance
Lightning Source LLC
LaVergne TN
LVHW050627100826
845148LV00011B/1767

* 9 7 8 1 6 3 2 9 6 4 6 8 7 *